THE HUMAN JOURNEY

Cover photo: Ossie Emery

Bruce Wilson

The Human Journey

CHRISTIANITY AND MODERN CONSCIOUSNESS

An Albatross Book

Published in Australia and New Zealand by
Albatross Books
P.O. Box 320, Sutherland
N.S.W. 2232, Australia
and in the United Kingdom by
Lion Publishing
Icknield Way, Tring
Herts HP23 4LE, England.

National Library of Australia Cataloguing-in-Publication data

Wilson, Bruce.
The human journey.

Simultaneously published, Tring, Eng.: Lion Publishing.
ISBN 0 86760 003 9
ISBN 0 85648 333 8 (Lion Publishing)

1. Theology, Doctrinal. I. Title.

230

Typeset in Sydney by Rochester Photosetting Service.
Printed in Singapore by Singapore National Printers (Pte) Ltd.

To

Zandra, Richard and Anthea
and my friend Don

Contents

Part Three: The Christian way

Part One:

The mystery of being human

1
Who am I?

THE SEARCH FOR PERSONAL IDENTITY

We have all caught our self looking at our self. Sometimes it happens in a very ordinary place like our own bathroom. We are looking into the mirror to brush our hair or shave, and we see our own eyes looking back at us. This is very strange. We stop brushing or shaving, and stare. We look at the face reflected in the mirror. Is this *me*? Our stare becomes an intent, puzzling gaze. Then for just a moment, at most a second or two, something even stranger happens. We become aware of both the self looking in the mirror and the self reflected in the mirror. It is as though there is a second self, a self outside space and time, which sees the self and its reflection in the mirror as one totality.

Sometimes this experience of the self which catches the self comes in moments of sheer wonder and delight. Perhaps we are standing at the top of a seaside cliff, staring across a vast expanse of blue water stretching to the horizon. Or perhaps we are in the country, staring across dappled fields to distant mountains, their peaks thrust defiantly skyward. Immensity and beauty hold our vision in fixed gaze. We thrill with the joy of being alive. Then, unexpectedly, we become aware of both the scene and our self viewing the scene. It is as though there is a self which can stand back from the view and the viewer, seeing them as one.

But sometimes this experience comes in moments of dread or nausea. Maybe we are walking across a paddock and we see a half-decayed animal carcass lying in the grass. Suddenly our imagination is filled with a picture of our own body lying there, also half-decayed. We are lifted above ourselves to see our self as a dead lump of brute matter, with consciousness evaporated to nothing.

By concentration these experiences can be reproduced at will. Focus fixedly on some material object, say a chair, and after a while, for just a few seconds, you will become aware of the chair and yourself looking at it. With practice the experience can be made to last longer, perhaps for half a minute or so.

The problem of identity

Let us call this second self which catches the self our *transcedent self*. 'Transcendent' seems to be the best word to describe it, because it appears to 'get above' normal things and ordinary experience. Most of us ignore our momentary experiences of the transcendent self, but I believe they are the clue to who we really are. We probably dismiss them through fear, for the transcendent self poses the dilemma of human identity: In this vast universe of matter and time, who am I? what am I? One great modern thinker began his journey into the problem of human identity when he realized he was a being who could ask this weird question: 'Why is there something and not nothing?'

We have many experiences which pose the problem of identity. Dreaming is one. Whether we are conscious of it or not, each of us dreams for several hours each night. It is even possible to dream that you are dreaming and to dream that you are awake. But let us take a simple example and see how it poses the problem of identity. Suppose you dream that you are a dog, then you awake (whatever that means!) and you begin to wonder whether waking is just a different kind of dreaming. Could it be possible that the *waking* self is really a dog dreaming it is a human being, just as the dreaming self was a human being dreaming it was a dog?

Admittedly all this is a bit silly: like the intellectual puzzles with which philosophy professors tease their new students. But there is something in it too. This sort of puzzle unveils the mystery of being human. Why do most people equate waking consciousness with reality and dream consciousness with unreality? Later we will have reason to look into dreams more seriously and sensibly. But now let us try to see how ordinary people usually cope with the problem of human identity.

Eva Adamson is not a real person, but in *Part One* of this book we will explore the problem of identity through the eyes of her experience. Eva is really two people. Sometimes she is terribly shallow — more like a caricature, a figure of fun, than a real person. This side of Eva represents the superficial identity many modern people are in danger of becoming. But sometimes Eva is all of us. She is the way we are made, the identity given to us through the process of growing up, or the identity for which we are still searching. The difference between the two Evas will be obvious. When we encounter the second Eva, it is important that we substitute our own life experiences for hers — our own sex roles, our own family, our own nationality etc.

Normal identity is usually no bother to us. Some sociologists call normal identity the *natural attitude* identity. They mean the taken-for-granted identity of ordinary, everyday life. Here we do not worry about dreams of transcendent selves. We feel we know who we are. It is not a problem, just a matter of common sense. Sometimes we might arrive at work or the breakfast table to be greeted by 'You're not looking yourself today', but we know nothing profound or disturbing is intended — although, if we are recovering from a hangover, the remark may make us more irritable.

One of the most powerful affirmations of normal identity are simple, everyday greetings like 'Good morning', 'Nice weather we're having' or 'How are you today?' All these assure us anew that we are just normal people living in a perfectly normal and ordinary world. One of the first things we do when meeting new people is to try to establish their 'natural attitude' identity. We ask them questions like, 'What work do you do?' or 'Where do you come from?' And we expect to answer similar questions in return.

But let us imagine that Eva Adamson is at a party where she meets someone who does not ask her these conventionally polite questions, but asks instead '*Who* are you?' Realizing that the questioner is serious and not playing some kind of game, we can suppose that Eva gives a 'natural attitude' reply:

> *I'm Eva Adamson. I'm thirty-four years old and I'm a housewife with two children. I live in Edena Gardens, which I suppose you could say is a nice middle-class suburb. We have lots of friendly neighbours. My father was in insurance until he retired and my husband Bill is a bank officer. I play golf twice a week, I like reading and I love to have friends for dinner or go out to a movie with Bill. On weekends we go sailing and take the kids to visit their grandparents. I suppose that will give you some idea of who I am!*

If this is all Eva can say about her identity, it is fairly shallow stuff. It is a bit like asking for meat and getting milk, or for wine and getting water. We can see the shallowness of mere 'natural attitude' identity by asking some deeper questions — questions which go beyond the ordinary everyday world and explore its reality roots. In the whole saga of human history, in the immensity of space and time, in the face of eternity and oblivion, who is Eva Adamson? Where did her life come from? Where will it go? What is this 'being alive'? Why is there a someone called Eva, and not no one or nothing? How is it that we are beings who can ask such awesome questions? Perhaps all this is a little abstract. Let us try to explore these questions in a concrete life-situation.

Suppose Eva's local parish priest calls on her. Now Eva has not been to church since she was a schoolgirl, except for weddings and funerals. But the priest has learnt from a neighbour that the Adamsons are Catholics. Over a cup of coffee the priest raises three questions with Eva. He asks her what the real purpose of her life is, what she thinks is going to happen to her when she dies and how she finds peace about guilt feelings. Eva admits that these questions are real enough — most people do — although she is not at all sure that she is grateful to the priest for raising them. (In a later chapter we will see what effect they have on her.)

A lot of people spend their lives trying to avoid questions about their ultimate identity. They try to live entirely in the 'natural attitude' self. There are many ways of achieving this. Some people make their everyday lives so busy, they never give themselves time to think about who they really are or what is the point of their endless activity. They are always working, planning a holiday, arranging a new purchase, watching television, playing sport, tinkering with the car or doing the garden. There is nothing 'wrong' with any of these activities in themselves — except when they are used to fill personal emptiness with busyness.

Other people see the problem of ultimate identity but, when it starts to gnaw at them, escape into some kind of soporific stupor. Alcohol is probably the most common, but today's doctors and psychiatrists are very obliging and will supply all kinds of anti-emptiness pills. This alternative is obviously more tragic than the first. It is often induced by the ageing process itself, especially with the arrival of the middle years of life when idealistic dreams have begun to fade and mortality starts to look real for the first time. But no one can avoid experiences which raise questions about their ultimate identity all of the time. Loneliness and death are two of the more common experiences which propel such questions into our consciousness.

A few years ago there was a popular song which touched on the connection between loneliness and ultimate identity. It was about a jet-set lady who lived in the phantasy world of cigarette advertisements. 'And where do you go, my lovely', the song asked, 'when you go home to your bed?' When the last champagne cork has popped, when the whoopees and the hurrahs of the pool party have died, in the dark of the night, *who* is she? And who are those who envy her life or would like to have her? Each of us is alone in the darkness of cosmic night. What is this little circle of lonely light we call our self?

And then there is death, that modern obscenity which must never be mentioned in front of the children. Our age suppresses the knowledge of death with all the fervour of Victorians suppressing the knowledge of sex. But no mortician's make-up can hide this cancer of the self. Every death — our parents', our neighbours', our friends' — reminds us of life's only certainty. What does it mean to live in the knowledge of death? What is the meaning of a universe which throws up a creature who can rise above its self to imagine its own death?

'Natural attitude' identity is shallow, but is there

anything better to put in its place? If there is not, then people who ask disturbing questions about identity should shut up and cease upsetting others unnecessarily. But we have already said that the transcendent self is the clue to who we really are. By looking deeply into this self, we will discover the answers to our deepest questions of identity. The curious thing is that the transcendent self is the cause of our problems in the first place. If we did not have it, we would live like all the other animals, perceiving and responding to the world of nature, but never rising above it. Questions about who we are, how to live, what to live for would not even occur to us.

Let there be no misunderstanding. Animals are wonderful creatures. Kindness to animals is a sure sign of a humane society. But we must not be so sentimental about our fellow creatures that we see only the features we share in common with them. Whenever human beings have left enough traces of their life-patterns for us to piece together something of what they thought, we discover they are always concerned with the dilemma of identity. So far as we are aware no animal, living or dead, has ever shown the least ability to pose questions about its identity. There is no cat art, dog philosophy or monkey religion. But art, philosophy and religion are always the mark of human life, however rudimentary. They are the mark of beings who possess a transcendent self, who are able to rise above themselves as well as nature. Perhaps one day another animal will start asking 'ultimate identity' questions, but that would only show it had come to possess a transcendent self too.

Exploring the transcendent self will reveal who we are. But first this journey must take one or two sidetracks. Often we do not realize we are on a sidetrack until we come to a dead end. There are a lot of people who imagine the sidetrack we are about to take is the main road to human identity! They are people who think that natural science can tell us who we really are.

2

Ghosts in the machine

MIND, MATTER AND THE UNIVERSE

Every piece of scientific work, from the biologist's research in the laboratory to the astronomer's at the radio-telescope, has two sides to it. They are so obvious that we generally take them for granted. Yet each aspect is quite crucial to the problem of human identity. First, there is the knowing person, the actual scientific *observer*. Second, there is the thing or things *observed*, that slice of reality being subjected to scientific scrutiny. Both aspects are necessary for science.

But, until recently, modern science has so concentrated on the 'out there' world of observation that it has almost forgotten the 'in here' person who does the observing. One result of this lop-sided emphasis is that the universe begins to look like a place where people do not fit. In this chapter we shall see why science cannot explain the ultimate identity of persons and how fatal it is to ignore the observing person.

The problem of chance and meaning

Today people who believe science can unlook the secret to the riddle of human identity are seldom scientists themselves. They are usually people who have benefited from the outstanding achievements of modern science — people for whom science has made life safer or wealthier, people who have seen science unlock many mysteries of the material universe. It is understandable that such people should come to expect science to unlock the mystery of being human too. In fact they already have a popular theory about human identity, based upon some of the ideas of a past generation of scientists. It goes roughly like this:

> *The human being is a complex electrical-chemical organism we call* homo-sapiens. *It is the accidental product of the evolution of matter and energy through an enormous passage of time.*

If we really believed this was true and we took it quite seriously (which is seldom the case with those who claim to believe it), then being human is an unfathomably tragic affair. Our personal self-consciousness, the part of the self we value most and the part that makes us truly human, becomes little more than a black joke played on us by the brute, insentient forces of matter and energy. Death would give personal self-consciousness about as much reality as an early morning mist. Fate, pure chance and unconscious matter become the ultimate roots of reality. Words like *love* and *trust* would lose all personal meaning and refer only to glandular secretions, or hormonal reactions. In these circumstances it would probably be better to forget about who we really are and get on with living in the natural attitude — as parents, golfers, moviegoers, bank officers, gardeners or whatever. Which is what a lot of people try to do. But can we really forget? Do we even, deep down, believe it anyway? Our emotions reject this explanation. Beautifully personal experiences, like making love or tucking our children into bed at night, make us feel there must be a better explanation to life than mere chance.

But there is no reason to believe this explanation anyway — it is self-contradictory. First, it tells us that we are electrical-chemical organisms, which is as obvious as saying bricks are made from clay. Then it says that these organisms have been aeons in the making. There is no problem here either — that is certainly the direction in which most of the scientific evidence points. But finally it claims that all this, and much more too, happened by pure accident. And here is the rub. If we are the products of undesigned chance, this must also include our minds (the knowing person). But if our minds are the product of an accident, how can we rely on them? How do we *know* that what our minds tell us is true — including the claim that our minds themselves came from chance? An illustration will make the point clearer.

Let us imagine that we take a roulette wheel and fill its spaces with all the letters of the alphabet and the numerals zero to nine. We then announce that we will spin this wheel until its stops spell out all of Shakespeare's plays and Einstein's theory of relativity. Now the odds against this happening are almost immeasurable. But that is not the point. Let us imagine that the wheel does in fact, through aeons of spinning, succeed on both counts. The point is how do we know it has succeeded? The answer is obvious. First, because we already have Shakespeare's plays and Einstein's theory before us — we know what is in them. Second, we ourselves (the knowing, observing experimenters) are the judge of the correct fit between what the wheel spells out and what Shakespeare and Einstein in fact wrote. Our ability to rise above the wheel on one hand and the writings of both authors on the other makes the test of fit or truth possible.

To claim that our minds are the accidental result of a purely material universe involves the following contradiction. To make this judgment, we must have some idea of reason and order, as well as chance and disorder — we must be able to 'rise above' both the chance universe and the chance minds that it supposedly threw up. Only then can we actually imagine what chance and disorder are. But how can we picture chance or disorder if our minds are just the product of pure chance? It is like asking the roulette wheel to decide for itself when it has reproduced Shakespeare and Einstein without having any idea of what is in Shakespeare or Einstein.

What we really need is an *explanation* that makes sense of both ourselves and the universe. Only this will give intelligibility to the apparent chance and disorder in the universe and of our mind's ability to 'rise above' this, and meaningfully interpret it. This explanation will have to wait until later chapters. Yet is is already obvious that there must be two levels of reality: one apparently dependent on chance and disorder, the other ordered and rational. Somehow human beings seem to participate in both worlds, which is a great source of confusion about who we really are.

Today's scientists are fully cognizant of the self-contradiction in the old explanations of human identity based on pure accident. This is why they have come to doubt the ability of natural science to ever unlock the ultimate mystery of human identity. They know that recent advances in the philosophy of science have shown that science itself is based on many unproved, perhaps unproveable, assumptions. Probably the most significant of these unproven assumptions is that the human mind is a reliable instrument for discovering truth.

It could be objected that all this talk about the human mind is too theoretical and airy fairy. I once had a conversation with a physicist who said just that. 'Look,' he argued, 'the minds we've got are all we've got and they work. They can discover truth. We've been able to show the earth is round, not flat, build computers and land a man on the moon. What further proof do you want?'

But he missed the point. Of course our minds are reliable; of course natural science works. But it is one thing to say that our minds are *reliable* and quite another to say that they derive from pure *chance*. My car's motor is reliable, our university computer is reliable, but chance did not produce them. How many of us would agree to ride in an aeroplane, where the pilot tossed dice to decide which control button he would press next? Those who say that pure chance produced the human mind are cutting away the only ground on which we could possibly believe them in the first place. They completely fail to explain the origin of the knowing mind which can tell the difference between order and disorder. They have made the discovery of truth impossible.

The problem of science and religion

In a moment we must look more deeply into the twin sides of science: the knowing person and the thing known. But first, we need to see another reason why many people look to science for the solution to the human identity dilemma.

Down the ages most human beings looked to religion for an explanation of identity. Mistrust of religion is a major reason why many look to science instead. This mistrust is largely derived from a battle between science and religion. The basic facts are well-known. Small skirmishes took place from the time of Copernicus, but all-out war was declared in the later part of last century over the question of human evolution. Christian literalists of the time insisted that the biblical account of creation must be taken at its face value. They said the universe was created in six days and anyone who claimed otherwise was an enemy of God himself. Science claimed the universe evolved over millions of years. Religion fought its case by appealing to authority and tradition but, because science appealed to reason and facts, science won.

Nowadays almost no leading scientist or theologian believes in the incompatibility of science and religion, not because science has disproved or displaced religion, but because each is seen to approach reality from different but equally valid sets of questions — just as an astronomer and a poet look at the moon from different perspectives. A great number of books have been written about science and religion; there is no wish to add this one to their number. Yet it is necessary to have a brief overview of the kind of peace that has developed. The main points can be summarized as follows.

Science is concerned with the *how, when* and *what* of things — about material facts and causes. Religion is concerned with the *why* — with meaning, purpose and knowing persons. Today's theologians say the biblical creation stories were never intended to give information about how or when the universe came into being; the fact that they are written as Hebrew poetry should have been evidence enough to avoid the mistake of thinking otherwise. Rather these stories tell about the place and condition of the personal in the universe — about human meaning, human purpose and tragedy; about the relationship of personal life to the ultimate origins of the universe. Of course there are scientists who do not accept the theological explanations of these stories. But it is not as scientists they reject them. They reject them, often quite amateurishly, as theologians or philosophers. And it is true to say that there are other scientists who accept the theological explanations equally amateurishly. It is silly to allow the prestige a scientist has earned in science to influence our judgments about his religious views, one way or the other. Often the religious opinions of a great scientist will be less profound than our postman's, despite the former's brilliant scientific mind.

The modern 'peace' between religion and science has not yet fully filtered down to the popular mind. Religion behaved so stupidly about science in the recent past that it still suffers from popular suspicion. We know religion rightly got a good knock on the head for attempting to suppress scientific discoveries, but does it have the clues to our real identity? Could we ever trust religion again? How can we trust something that blatantly used power, authority and tradition to suppress facts it did not like?

Yet most of us feel that there must be a better explanation of identity than chance and matter. This is the double bind which causes so many people to run away from the problem about ultimate identity. Science either cannot give the answers, or the answers it does give seem too small to fit all the facts of our experience. Religion, on the other hand, is not trusted because it does not appear to be based in reality, just authority and tradition.

The twin sides of science

Further reflection on the way science actually works might help us find a way out of this impasse. Earlier we noted that science assumes, but otherwise tends to ignore, the knowing person side of scientific endeavour. The result is that persons start to look like aliens trapped in an immense, impersonal machine.

Imagine a dog which, from a tiny puppy, has spent its whole life solely in the company of chickens. It probably thinks it is a chicken itself. But some facts about its own being do not fit the reality. No matter how hard it tries, it can never lay an egg or fly up on to a roost. Until it found another dog, it could never quite feel that the world had a proper place for creatures like it. This is what happens to human beings when they spend all their time looking at the material universe and forget about the people who do the looking. The world starts to seem like a place where persons do not fit. It is the aim of this book to correct the imbalance a little — to concentrate our attention on the knowing person. We might then begin to discover who we really are. We might even begin to find that religion has a basis in reality, not just authority or tradition.

At first sight modern science appears to enormously reduce the significance of being human. By greatly enlarging our knowledge about the size of the universe, astronomy makes our own planet look less than a grain of sand. And if the earth is less than a grain of sand, what are we, its tiny inhabitants? Modern scientific discovery has reduced our significance in time as well as space. If the whole history of the universe was recorded as a full length feature movie, the complete history of the human race would probably occupy about two frames. Our own individual lifetime would be so insignificant it would not appear at all.

But suppose we turn things around and focus on the knowing person *here* instead of the immensity of time and space *out there*. Now we see something very strange: the immensity of time and space is not only 'out there' but also 'in here' in our own minds, in our consciousness. This is even clearer when we divide the experience into its component parts. First, our self-consciousness sees the immensity of the space-time universe. Second, it sees its own body and lifespan as a tiny part of that immensity. Third, it sees that, in order to make such a comparison, it itself must rise above both. At the third stage we encounter a fantastic being who is and in some way is not (temporarily at least) part of space and time. One part of the knowing person appears to be like a mirror or telescope which simply reflects an image of the vast 'out there' universe. We can call this part of us our *consciousness*: other animals seem to possess it too. But another part 'rises above' this reflection, circling as it were all around it, evaluating, comparing, trying to understand and work it all out. This part of consciousness seems to have its own particular kind of vastness — in some degree to be outside space and time altogether. We can call this part our *self-consciousness*, or the transcendent self. So far as we know, the transcendent self is uniquely human.

Another equally fantastic dimension of the transcendent self is its creativity. Somehow it can make links between things it has never actually seen linked together before. Thus a great scientist like Einstein predicted how to split the atom and convert matter into energy by the mere mathematical equations he worked out in his own mind. It is quite mistaken to view the transcendent self simply as a reality-receptor, like some kind of sophisticated computer, camera or tape-recorder. In some cases at least, it clearly contributes to what we call reality, and does not merely receive it. Time is a good example. We measure time by movement and change — the changing seasons, ageing, orbital movements, mechanical movements, electronic pulsations etc. But try to imagine time in a universe without self-conscious beings in it. It is impossible. All we can imagine is movement and change, the phenomena we use to measure time. Time is a personal dimension of reality, a product of beings like us who not only grow older but who know that they grow older. Time seems to be part of our ability to 'stand back' and watch movement and change in the universe, including the changes in our own bodies we call 'ageing'. Time seems to have close links with our ability to rise above our self and imagine our own death.

We can see that the knowing person who gets above simple stimulus and response is just as important a part of reality as the 'out there' universe. Any explanation of human identity which ignores the knowing person is falsely lop-sided.

But what is this transcendent self which rises above both the space-time universe and our consciousness of that universe? Those who believe the second or self-conscious self is just a chance product of matter and energy, a sort of cosmic hiccup, will find modern science simply adds to their despair about life's ultimate futility and insignificance. But without the transcendent self there would be no science. Animals have consciousness, but not self-consciousness: hence they have no science either. Our ability to rise above nature and the self is the very foundation of our science. Animals appear to be locked into a closed stimulus-response universe. Of course that is part of our world too, but only part. Any attempt to explain the transcendent self by stimulus and response is self-contradictory.

Suppose someone says the transcendent self is totally dependent upon brain chemistry. How does brain chemistry 'get above' itself to know that it is just brain chemistry? Now there is obviously a close relationship between brain chemistry and the transcendent self, similar perhaps to the relationship between the light source and the lens of a movie projector. If you crack or scratch the lens, you will distort the image projected by the light source. What is denied is that the transcendent self is just brain chemistry. Or suppose someone tries to explain the transcendent self by claiming it is only one half of the brain reflecting on the experience of the other half. How does that person 'get above' both halves of his/her own brain to make this claim, and how do we in order to believe it?

Damage to the brain clearly limits the function of the transcendent self, but a normal brain may limit it too. Perhaps there is a transcendent self which exists with an immense brain far less limiting than our own. Or perhaps there is a transcendent self which exists without the limitation of any kind of space-time body or brain at all. Obviously we would want good evidence before we could believe in such beings or Being.

For us the transcendent self appears to be some kind of hole in an otherwise closed matter-energy universe. Our dilemma about identity springs from the difficulty of knowing whether this gap is a passing phase — the cosmic hiccup theory again — or a door into another kind of reality altogether. Because natural science simply assumes the knowing person as part of its investigative apparatus, we cannot expect it to solve the problem for us. But social science studies human beings and many people believe that it has the answers. So let us make this the next stop on our journey.

3

Robed apes and naked humans

IDENTITY AND SOCIAL SCIENCE 1

Imagine a baby that is somehow reared without any human contact. This is an experiment we can only conduct in imagination; to do it in reality would be cruel and inhuman. But let us suppose that a pregnant woman has got lost in some remote, deserted part of the earth. She gives birth, but dies an hour afterwards. Her baby survives and is discovered by wild animals, let us say monkeys. Stretching our imagination further, we shall suppose that the baby reaches the age of twenty before we discover him on an exploring expedition. What would he be like?

He would probably have a scruffy beard, long hair, dirty fingernails — but he would look recognizably human. Although perhaps a bit stunted through undernourishment, physically he would be the same as you and me. But *psychically* he would hardly be human at all. In all likelihood he would think of himself as a monkey. Having seen his own reflection in a pool of water and noticing his relatively hairless arms and legs, he would probably think he is a deformed monkey. Certainly when it comes to climbing trees, his feet would be useless compared to the monkeys'. But we are already beginning to project a humanity on to him which he does not have. We are assuming that he can think like us, but he cannot.

At best the 'monkey boy' may have a dim, dull awareness of himself as different from the other monkeys. To think, you have to have a language, and he does not have one. Oh yes, he may respond to a shrill monkey shriek that warns of approaching danger, or make a happy chuckling sound every time he finds a fruit-laden banana tree. But in the normal sense he does not have a language and therefore does not think. He has a brain like yours and mine, but no *mind*. He can probably only just distinguish himself from the nature which surrounds him. He is much better than you and I at picking up all sorts of cues from the natural world around him — bird cries, subtle indications of weather changes, the smell of different types of foliage. But his self-consciousness is probably about as clear as ours when we first emerge from the effects of an anaesthetic after a surgical operation.

The point of this imaginary experiment is to show how much of what we are — our identity — depends on being part of a human group — a society and culture. Today in the Western world, a lot of people mistakenly overemphasize their individuality because they fail to realize that 'being human' means 'being part of a human group'. To be fully human one must not only have a body which is part of nature, but also a psyche which is part of human history and society. If pressed to put a figure on it, I would hazard a guess that ninety-nine per cent of what we call our individuality is actually the product of the human groups in which we were reared and one per cent the product of individual psyche or self. Perhaps this is a slight exaggeration, but often an exaggeration is necessary when the truth has been bent too far in the other direction.

The perspective of social science

The last one hundred years or so have seen the development of numerous ways of trying to understand how the human psyche is constructed. So far this study, which goes under the name 'social science', is fairly rough and ready compared to the achievements of the natural sciences. But many advances have been made. Psychiatry, psychology and sociology are probably the better known social sciences. Some of their specialized jargon, like 'inferiority complex' or 'unconscious motives', has already become part of popular thinking and speech.

But can the social sciences explain who we ultimately are? Can they solve the problems of human identity? Obviously many people think they can. Just think, for example, about the huge number of popular books on psychology or sociology and the enormous enrolments in social science courses at universities and colleges. As well there is the growing number of people seeking psycho-analysis or psychiatric counselling. In some parts of the world it is becoming almost as necessary to have your own analyst as your own toothbrush. These are just some indicators of the growing belief that social science is the answer — but is it? Let us explore the matter for ourselves.

Let us go back to Eva Adamson again, back to her childhood. This is the period of life where psychology has done most of its work. Please remember that I am only interested in Eva's childhood so far as it directly relates to the matter of human identity. Sex aside, Eva is physically no different from the monkey boy. But Eva is going to be reared in a human family. In the first few years of life she will learn a language. First 'Mumma' or 'Dadda', then 'babee', 'pottee' and so on. Soon she will be speaking in sentences. The whole process is so normal and natural that most people never even imagine the depths of what is actually happening. Eva is learning to describe the world — to give names to everything from teddy bears and cots to puppy dogs and motor cars, just like the Bible's story of creation where God tells Adam to give names to all the other creatures. Language is beginning to 'lift' Eva up out of her immersion in the world of things. Language is starting to put a mental *space* between her self and the rest of reality. Through learning a language, Eva is beginning to acquire a mind, whereas the monkey boy's self remained immersed in nature because there was no one to teach him a language.

But even more significant and complex things are happening. Eva is beginning to see that reality has different kinds of being in it. She discovers that some parts of her world are just like her — they have minds too. Soon she learns to distinguish between these types of being. She discovers that she is a *me*, a little window on the whole universe out there. She will feel that her *me* is 'in here', while other things are 'out there'. She will also discover that most of the 'out there' things do not have a 'me in here' inside them like she has. Rocks, trees, motor cars, teddy bears — in fact anything which does not seem to have this feeling of 'me in here' inside it — she will regard as an *it*. Sometimes her mother and father will have lots of fun with Eva by pretending that an *it* does have a 'me in here' inside it. They will make her teddy bear or a doll speak like a human, and Eva will giggle and laugh. But the whole sense of fun depends on the fact that Eva knows it is only a game — knows that teddy bears do not really have a *me* inside them.

Even when Eva is a grown woman she may not consciously understand all these things that have happened to her. They will have become part of the world she takes for granted, the same way she takes her kidneys or liver for granted — unless they give her trouble. But identity has begun to give modern people trouble. That is why we need to understand how human identity is constructed.

When she has learnt to speak in sentences, Eva will say things like, 'Evie thirsty, Mummy; please give Evie some milk'. And her mere vocalizing of these sound symbols will get a response from her mother. Perhaps this will be in the form of more sound symbols like, 'Not just now Eva, I'm busy'. Or maybe the response will be mother going to the refrigerator and pouring her a glass of milk. Eva has been able to recognize her biological need (thirst), create a picture in her little mind of something to satisfy it (milk), and turn that need and picture into sound symbols ('Evie thirsty; milk please, Mummy').

If she could think about it deeply, Eva would realize that the sound symbols must stir up similar pictures in her mother's mind because her mother makes a meaningful response. So Eva learns that her mother has a 'me in here' inside her too. She learns that human body shapes are not just an *it*, even though they are 'out there' like an *it*. They are like a *me*, but one which is 'out there' rather than 'in here' like her own. Eva would probably just call them 'other people' but, because I need to be more precise, we shall call them a *you*. So we have three types of being: *me*, *it* and *you*.

By now you will realize why I said that the monkey boy could have barely distinguished himself from nature. For although he had the same bodily equipment as Eva, he needed language and another human person before he could properly realize the difference between 'me in here', 'it out there' and 'you out there'. You may be thinking that he could have solved this difficulty by inventing his own language. Perhaps he could have invented a very rudimentary language — a grunt for this, a groan for that — but it would not have changed much, because language works by using symbols to transfer pictures and ideas from one mind to another.

Let us suppose that by himself he invented a system of sounds which had the meaning to him of 'Do you think it will rain today?' The monkey boy goes up to one of his monkey brothers and asks this question. But to his monkey brother they are just sounds because, so far as we know, even though they have probably been around longer than us, monkeys do not have the right equipment for linking symbols and impressions of reality together into a language.

Until the monkey boy became aware of other beings who had similar pictures in their heads as he had in his, and until those pictures were tossed back and forth in conversation, he would remain trapped in nature as if it was a dream. In fact 'dream' is precisely the right word. For the way we distinguish 'reality' from phantasy* or dreams is through being aware that other people see the same things we see. One morning recently my wife asked me if I had bought a new suit, or whether she had just dreamt that I had. I assured her that I had not bought a new suit, that I could not even afford to buy one and that, although I wished it was true, she must have been dreaming. Phantasy and dreams appear to us as our own private world. Only by sharing our pictures of the world with other people can we 'rise above' nature and distinguish it from phantasy and dreams. That is why people who spend long periods totally alone, like lone sailors circumnavigating the globe, report experiences of hallucination and the fear of insanity. They are beginning to lose the ability to distinguish between dream consciousness and reality consciousness. You can imagine how

* Throughout this book the word 'phantasy' is used in the Freudian sense of psychic or mental projections. The occasional use of the more common word 'fantasy' has the popular meaning of 'amazement' or 'wonder'.

someone like the monkey boy, who has always lived alone, never even develops this ability.

We can now see how social psychology has unravelled much of the mystery surrounding the origins of mind and self. Its explanation is quite naturalistic, and therefore rather disturbing to people who previously thought of this part of the self in purely religious terms as soul or spirit. For what seemed like total mystery turns out to be the consequence of language and human relationships. Presumably the only other equipment one needs is the right anatomy — a human voice box to speak, a human ear to hear and a human brain to code and decode language.

Self-consciousness and the 'I'

This is where a lot of people would like to leave off. 'We have now explained human identity', they think. 'It is all just a matter of stimulus and response, like a computer, but a little more complicated than we first expected — with all this language and human relationship business.' The technical name for people who hold this view is *behaviourists*.

But there is still at least one other type of being which we have not mentioned yet. Apply what has been said in this chapter to me the writer (or to yourself the reader). So far I have explained how a person like me comes to have a sense of myself (me) as different from things (it) and other persons (you). But note: *I* have explained my self and my mind. You see I am not just a *me*, but also an *I*. Inside my consciousness there is an inner conversation going on all the time between these two parts of the self — the *I* and the *me*. And the *I* is the more fundamental part of consciousness; without it we could never 'get above' ourselves to see the *me*. Self-consciousness depends upon this inner dialogue of the two selves. So now we have four types of being: *me, it, you* and *I*.

The *me* part of the self is what social science studies. Like natural science, it simply assumes the knowing person — the *I* part of the self. Sometimes social science looks at an individual *me* (psychology and psychiatry) and sometimes at a *me* as part of a human group — *me* and *you* (social psychology and sociology). Natural science deals with the *it* part of reality, including the human body (anatomy, biology, physiology etc.). Of course these divisions are only made for convenience — to cope with the difficulty involved in one person trying to master them all. Most of us cannot even master one of them. But reality itself is interrelated, so sometimes natural science and social science try to get together. For example, physiological psychology seeks to understand the relationship between the body and the psyche.

But what is the *I* — the knowing, transcending self which all the sciences assume and take for granted? Without it there would be no science at all, natural or social. Here once again we have come up against the hard, irreducible fact of the transcendent self. But what is it? Does the transcendent self just float above everything else in a sea of nothingness? Is it merely a waste product of the material universe, as it were — a piece of cosmic flotsam — or is it part of another, nonmaterial reality? Religion, of course, claims that this is *exactly* what it is — part of a nonmaterial, spiritual reality. 'If instead of looking "out there" all the time,' says religion, 'we began to look "in and through" again, we would discover yet another type of being — spiritual being'.

Before we look at the claims of religion, there are a couple of other tracks we must explore. Yet already we can say that, whatever it is, we know that the *I* is the most real part of the person — which makes it more than a little strange that today people pay it such scant attention.

4

The computer program self

IDENTITY AND SOCIAL SCIENCE 2

In the last chapter we saw the human mind and self in the process of construction. But it was just a bare identity, a skeleton without flesh. Now we must go further and see how that identity acquires a body — how it gets fleshed out into a full human person. Once again I want to tell the story through the life experiences of Eva Adamson.

This time we need to go further back than Eva's childhood, right back to the day she was born. There she is, still wet and purple, howling out her little lungs in the obstetrician's arms: not Eva Adamson yet — that won't happen until she marries Bill in twenty-three years' time — but Eva Reilly. The year is 1946 and the place a maternity hospital in Sydney, Australia. John Reilly, Eva's father, is an insurance salesman. Her mother, June, was a schoolteacher until she fell pregnant with Eva. John Reilly's great-grandfather, an Irish Catholic, emigrated to Australia during the gold rush of the

1850s. June Reilly's family came to Australia from England after the great European War of 1914-18.

So you can see Eva is already destined to become a European, English-speaking, middle-class, Roman Catholic, Australian citizen. Needless to say, this is a very large slice of what Eva will come to regard, almost unawares, as her personal identity. We can easily imagine that if the birth scene had been somewhere quite different, say Calcutta India, with Brahmin notables as parents, then Eva's self-identity would be destined to take a very different shape indeed.

The social self and the influence of culture

Eva has not only been born into the world of nature, but also into a world of human society and culture. With a lot of ingenuity and experiment the monkey boy, of whom we spoke in the last chapter, may have invented a hooked stick to pull bananas from trees. But in Eva's world there is already a highly developed human technology. Before she was born, people were washing their clothes in machines, flying through the air in aeroplanes and listening to radio descriptions of cricket matches being played twenty thousand kilometres away in England. (Remember it is only 1946.) The monkey boy may have learnt to recognize a particular monkey shriek as a sign of danger. But by the time Eva is twenty, she will have learnt to read and write English, and perhaps another language as well. She has been born into a pre-existing human culture.

As a young adult she can play Beethoven on the family hi-fi set, eat with a knife and fork, wear pantyhose, say her church catechism and solve geometry problems. Eva is like a highly sophisticated computer being programmed by her family, school, university and church, by magazines, books, radio and television. Crammed into this computer will be thousands of years of human experience, knowledge, wisdom and, of course, nonsense. To change the simile, Eva's self will be like the crest of a huge human tidal wave, composed of the ancestral thought and traditions of her forbears. This, by the way, is probably why some societies have mistakenly believed that their ancestors were all around them as spirits, demanding homage and worship. Our ancestors are all around us, but only in the sense that our cultural tradition passes their ideas and habits into our minds through the process which sociologists call socialization.

Our fleshed-out self is the product of society and culture, of a human world that was there before we were born. This is the world of human science, technology, manners, morals, customs, economics, politics, art, religion and philosophy. History is the social science which tries to make sense of that pre-existing world — to understand the past. What memory is to the individual self, history is to the social self. Without memory we could not make much sense of our personal identities. If a person could not remember, say, that when he was a teenager old Uncle Joe had left his father a small fortune, then he would not understand how he had acquired his present taste for caviar and other luxuries.

Sometimes psychiatrists have to 'mine' forgotten

memories and bring them to the surface, in order to help their patients redirect an unhappy personality trait. For example, a patient may have consulted an analyst about claustrophobia and, with the analyst's help, he discovers long-forgotten memories of being locked in a broom cupboard as a small child. But neither can we make much sense of our personal identities unless we can remember the story of our group or groups. For just as it is true that man makes history, so it is also true that history makes man.

When I was a child two buses took children to the local schools from the area where my family lived. One bus went to the Roman Catholic and the other to the State school. If our bus came first, we would rush inside, open the windows and yell 'Tyke bastards', spitting on the Catholic children still waiting at the bus stop. If their bus came first the whole scene reversed, except that the derision 'Protestant buggers' now accompanied the expectoration. Not one of us, nor I suspect most of our parents, had more than a vague idea of the theological beliefs that divided us. We had even less idea of that expansive Christian vision of reality shared by Protestant and Catholic alike. It never even occurred to us that we were simply playing out anew the traditional enmity between our English Protestant and Irish Catholic forbears.

History had made us — and not especially polite nor understanding — but we did not know it. Similarly we cannot understand our 'human-constructed' identities unless we also know how history has shaped the particular groups in which we have been reared — family, social class, nationality.

Anthropology and sociology have greatly enlarged our knowledge of these areas of life.

In Australia a working-class family is not usually over-fussed if an unmarried daughter falls pregnant. They tend to take it in their stride. Often the girl's mother will accept and rear the new baby as if it were her own. But if the son of a working-class family turns out to be homosexual then, so far as his family is concerned, he might as well drop dead. Upper-class families tend to be the opposite. They find it rather entertaining to have a homosexual son. But a pregnant, unmarried daughter will be hurried interstate for an eight-month 'working' holiday or be quickly and expensively aborted in a flurry of anger and shame. Australian middle-class families tend to have apoplexy on either account.

Now I am not trying to be flippant, nor am I making any moral judgment. My only point is to show how social class affects the way we think and behave, and how groups within larger groups, in this case family and social class within Australian society, shape our identities.

Identity and the difference between cultures

Another method social science uses to demonstrate how the experience of particular groups shapes our identity is cultural comparison. The early history of Australia provides a fine example. It was marked by continuous hostility between the white British colonizers and the black Aborigines who had occupied the country for centuries. Because of Australia's vast, semi-arid hinterland, sheep grazing became the most profitable occupation for the white settlers. But as the graziers moved further inland, they and their shepherds came under Aboriginal attack. The whites interpreted this an unprovoked savagery. It confirmed their view that Aborigines were little more than wild animals. 'There is plenty of land', the graziers argued. 'Why don't the Aborigines just move away from the sheep pastures?'

But more recently anthropologists have shown that these lands were sacred to the Aborigines: each tribe had its own territory protected, the blacks believed, by spiritual powers. To venture into another tribe's sacred territory invited the wrath of its spiritual protector and a just death at the hands of its rightful occupiers. This sacral-social system was very sophisticated, developed over thousands of years. By forcing the Aborigines out of their sacred territories, the whites were destroying their social and spiritual identity. Occasionally the whites had vague inklings about what was happening, but they dismissed it all as childish superstition. Usually they did not understand at all. Aboriginal identity and British identity had been formed in very different melting pots indeed.

Thus we can see that social science not only explains how we acquire a mind and a self, but also how we acquire the *contents* of that mind and self, well most of the contents anyway. (It could only be 'most' and not 'all', otherwise we could not account for change — for new ideas, new inventions, religions, morals etc.) The fact that human beings are not just the products of their social and cultural environment is proven by the existence of social and cultural change. We are not only made by our history; we also make history ourselves. The human world that was there before we were born can be changed by us and handed on anew to the next generation. Apart from the slow mutations of biological evolution, animals repeat the same life-patterns over and over again, generation after generation. By contrast human life is characterized by change — by political, religious and technological revolutions which transform both the past and the future.

Somewhere within human beings there is a self which can 'stand outside' its own social and cultural environment — a self which is the source of creativity and freedom. Whatever it is, again I suggest that we call this self the transcendent self. Without it human beings could not have a history — they would not be alike to 'rise above' their socio-cultural environment, either to see what made them or to see how they might make themselves differently.

As you have read about the social science explanation of identity in this chapter, another piece of evidence pointing to the reality of the transcendent self has emerged: in yourself. Think about your own reaction to what has been said. Perhaps you have never thought much about these things before but, even if you have, I expect that your reaction will be much the same. You probably feel unnerved, even a little threatened, or at least a bit giddy about all the implications. Your self-identity now appears to be quite relative to the time and circumstances of your birth and upbringing. This may cause you to wonder, even to worry, about the validity of meanings and moral values you hold very dearly — things that seem part and parcel of your own personal identity. You may also be wondering about how free you really are, feeling perhaps like a television set that has only received one or two channels all its life. You may be doubting whether it is possible to find personal truth at all. Perhaps you feel tempted to give up the search for an authentic identity and just live for today or for kicks.

But these reactions ignore a deeper level of your experience. That self which is worried about freedom and truth, worried about authentic identity, has transcended the self which is a mere product of our social and cultural environment. If we never got above the self of upbringing and environment, we could never test the reality of that self; we could never separate prejudice and old wives' tales from fairness and truth. The transcendent self is not only the core of human being, but also that part of the self which is capable of exercising freedom of choice and of discovering truth. It 'rises above' both the world of nature and the world of human society and culture. At the moment you may feel that it is a very rootless self, causing you to experience fear, anxiety, or confusion. Such feelings are to be expected. In the next chapter, we will be examining one modern way of trying to solve them.*

* There is one very great social scientist (Karl Marx) who, in attempting to maintain his wholly naturalistic view of life, has engaged in a piece of verbal deception. Faced with the obvious fact that humans are self-conscious beings and that they do change the

world, he will not admit to the reality of a transcendent self as such. Instead, he explains these things by saying that human beings are that specific part of nature wherein nature comes to know itself.

But how does nature come to know itself? Some parts of reality seem to be totally unconscious (e.g. rocks and sand); others seem less and more conscious (e.g. plants and animals). But so far as we know, only human beings are self-conscious — only human beings know nature — and know that they know it too. No other part of reality, except human beings, seems to have the capacity to transcend itself.

The great appeal of Marxism today stems from the fact that it has synthesized the discoveries of modern natural and social science into one great system. But it fails to explain the most important reality of all — the personal, knowing transcendent self. That is why in practice Marxism has turned out to be so oppressive of human freedom and so cruel to individual persons.

5

The insane self

IDENTITY AND MENTAL ILLNESS

Who am I? What is this being alive? What shall I live for? What shall I live by? What will happen to me when I die?

It is clear by now that these ultimate questions are asked by that part of our self which we have called the transcendent self. They are peculiarly human questions; rocks, trees, ink-wells and rabbits do not ask them. We human beings ask them, because in some sense or other we 'get above' our space-time environment. Our journey into the sciences has only deepened the mystery about who we really are, because science itself depends upon this self that 'gets outside' of everything else.

At the end of chapter 3 we noted that the transcendent self is paid scant attention by people today. I said that this was 'strange'. But there are those who think it strange that someone should actually explore this self and its harrowing questions at all. They regard such people not as being 'outside' but 'beside' themselves — in a word, crazy. They characterize those of us who look for answers to these ultimate questions as morbid or mentally disturbed souls needing psychiatric treatment. They want to try to keep all explanations of human identity within the boundary of everyday life, the space-time universe. They regard the ultimate questions themselves as symptoms of mental illness or disturbance. Let us try to follow the tricky paths of this most recent of modern attempts to cope with the mystery of human identity.

Ultimate questions and mental sickness

It is generally agreed that ultimate questions have been the central concern of all great religious teachers. It follows then that, if these questions and the people who ask them are sick, all our great religious teachers have been mentally deranged. Exactly this view was taken by a lecturer in psychiatry at a university where I used to work. Lecturing to medical students, she would insist that Jesus Christ was a schizophrenic. I often wondered whether she would have prescribed crucifixion or electro-convulsive therapy — and which was the worst! Perhaps you feel that she was going a bit too far. On the contrary, my own opinion is that she was drawing the logical conclusion to a very popular modern attitude. I want to describe this attitude through the experience of Eva Adamson.

In chapter 1 we imagined Eva receiving a visit from her local parish priest. Like so many people today, Eva did not consider herself to be religious. It is true that she would say prayers with her children some nights, asking God to bless Grandma, Grandad and the cat, but it was more from a habit learnt in her own childhood than from any theological beliefs she could explain. The fact is that throughout her adult life Eva has hardly given one serious thought to religion. She regards herself as a very 'with it' kind of person, and religion as staid and old-fashioned. However you will recall that the priest challenged Eva with three questions: one about the meaning of her life, another about death and what lies beyond it, and another about guilt. Let us now suppose that after this visit, Eva begins to change.

At first Eva gets depressed a lot more than she used to. Her neighbours start to whisper behind her back: 'She's not the life of the party anymore — what's up with her?' Among her close friends wonder is already giving way to serious concern. Eva's husband, Bill, has been confiding with them about her recent strange behaviour. He says that she is always asking, 'What's the point of it all, why are we all here?' Bill just cannot understand her. He says that he keeps reminding her of 'all the good things she's got going for her', but it makes no difference.

'I adore her myself', he comments. 'She's got two beautiful, healthy children, a lovely house, nice friends, her own car — what *more* does she want?' With anguish Bill says, 'I wasn't even able to break her out of it when I suggested we go overseas for a holiday. And what's more,' he continues, 'she's starting to rake over the past, especially that quarrel which caused the break with her mother four years ago'.

Bill feels that he is beginning to get to his wit's end. 'Do you know,' he declares insistently, 'sometimes I catch her sitting at the kitchen table just thinking — just *thinking* — when the dishes haven't been done or the kids' beds made'.

But what upsets Bill most is that 'she keeps wondering about death all the time, and she's only thirty-four next birthday'. He thinks Eva might still be upset about Sally, her old school-friend who lost a breast to cancer a couple of months back.

'But that was just bad luck and, anyway, it's not likely to strike so close again for a while at our age. But maybe she does need to see a doctor', he quietly adds.

Is Eva really sick? Has the priest induced in her a morbidity which, as her husband and friends are beginning to say, should cause her to seek psychiatric help? Please do not misunderstand the point I am making. I think everyone would agree that if she kept asking these questions, without ever seeking or finding answers to them, Eva would become very sick indeed. She would collapse physically and mentally. But that is not the point. The point is whether she is sick in asking such questions in the first place — whether the questions themselves are symptomatic of mental illness. Before I ask you to decide, I would like to contrast Eva's experience with that of another person.

Suppose I have a friend who, although he lives in an eleventh-floor flat, always insists on using the stairs instead of the lifts. Suppose also that he continually complains of headaches and other aches and pains, though his doctor, after every conceivable radiological and pathological test, can find nothing physically wrong with him. And suppose that he repeatedly takes days off work, complaining of illness, and that on those days he suffers from severe bouts of depression.

I think you would agree that he is neurotic — that he is suffering from claustrophobia and hypochondria. And would I not be right to suspect that he had suffered some kind of childhood trauma, that his marriage was unhappy, or that he had sex problems? Because most people do not have his strange, self-hurting behaviour, I try to explain it in terms of his own particular life story or, better still, leave it to his psychiatrist to explain it. But whoever explains my friend's little oddities, and perhaps he will even work them out for himself one day, they will have to 'dig into' his own unique biography. For his problems are very much his own. Most of us are not afraid to ride in lifts. And, thankfully, most of us are not constantly subject to vague aches and pains when there is no physical cause.

Now we must try to decide whether Eva is mentally ill or not. What do you think? I wonder if you can see any important difference between my friend's dilemma and Eva's? My own opinion is that Eva is not mentally ill, and that the contrast with my friend's case shows why. Their problems are significantly different. Eva's do not derive from her own special biography; they are human problems — everybody has them. For however hard we try to push it to the back of our minds, all of us are concerned about the purpose of life — concerned to know whether we are part of some eternal plan, or just the jetsam of time and matter. And all of us wonder about death. Is it nothingness, or is there another life when we shall see our families and friends again?

You may not be quite so convinced that guilt is also a universal human problem. We will have to look at this matter in more depth later. But do you know anybody who completely lives up to the moral standards they themselves believe in?

Two types of personal problems

This matter of sickness and its relationship to ultimate questions needs clarifying in a little more detail. We need to distinguish between two kinds of personal problems faced by human beings. I shall call them *neurotic* problems and *existential* problems.

Neurotic problems are the ones that stem from our own particular life histories. They are like the problems my friend has. Very often the experiences which cause the damage will come from relationships with our parents in childhood and early adolescence, or from sexual difficulties. More often than not, neurotic problems will also be associated with some kind of social deprivation: poverty, inadequate education, loneliness, unemployment and so on. Because of this 'social connection', we should not be surprised to find that people with similar life experiences have similar neurotic problems.

But neurotic problems are not part and parcel of the condition of every human being as such. And, because they have human causes, neurotic problems can in principle be solved by human action. Currently we try to solve them with counselling, psycho-analysis, drug therapy, social reforms and social revolution. With some justification, we think of neurotic problems as the rightful concern of experts like psychiatrists, psychologists, social workers and sociologists, and of non-experts like reformers, moralizers and — in some circumstances — revolutionaries.

Existential problems are *givens* of human existence; everybody has them — including psychiatrists and psychologists. They are part and parcel of the condition of every human being. They are not contingent upon particular family, social or sexual experiences. Eva's priest summarized these existential problems when he challenged her to face the three questions about meaning, death and guilt. In other words, existential problems are the same as ultimate questions. I have temporarily changed the name in order to emphasize that these questions are givens of human existence. To be human is to have these problems.

The confused state of modern thinking has lumped these two types of problems together and regarded both as symptoms of mental illness. Thus when people like Eva get disturbed about existential problems, we send them off to psychiatrists or other mental health specialists. Because these specialists often share the same confusion too, they tend to accept existential problems as symptoms of mental disorder. Of course a lot of their patients have a combination of neurotic and existential problems. In this book I have no intention of debating whether neurotic problems themselves should be called 'sick'. Some people believe that the word 'sick' should be applied to the circumstances which produced the problem and not to the person who has it. But I do want to insist that existential problems should not be regarded as symptoms of mental illness.

To call someone 'sick' we have to compare their condition with examples of health — people who are well. This can be done with neurotic problems. For although every one of us suffers from some kind of neurotic problem or other, we do not all suffer from the same problem. Some of us have a nervous twitch and some do not and so on. But all of us experience existential problems — this is 'normal'.

Let us consider what happens when existential problems are treated as signs of mental illness. Suppose that Eva takes her husband and friends' advice and consults a psychiatrist. What 'treatment' will she get for her ultimate questions? Probably something between the following two extremes. On the one hand the psychiatrist might use drug therapy. He might give her drugs to calm her down, to relieve the depression, to stop her from thinking too much or too clearly — or to stop her from thinking at all. This would not be an exceptional treatment today. It does not solve the problems, but it does prevent us from being aware of them.

On the other hand, the psychiatrist might counsel Eva in individual or group therapy sessions. Forgetting that he himself had the same problems, the psychiatrist would be searching for the cause of Eva's ultimate question symptoms in her own unique biography. For the reason I have already given, this is an exercise with as much promise of success as looking for pots of gold at the end of rainbows.

Most psychiatrists would probably use some kind of combination of these 'therapies'. But what would be their ultimate aim? This is easy to answer, because it would be the same in every case. The aim would be to bring Eva back to the situation where she was not troubled by ultimate questions: where she did not ask about the purpose of life, where she suppressed all intimations of her personal mortality, where she either swallowed her guilt into her unconsciousness or tried to convince herself that she did not feel any guilt anyway. In other words, the aim would be to make Eva again the woman for whom the 'natural attitude' is the only reality — the everyday round, plus parties and holidays. Back to the woman who knows she is just a housewife with two children and a husband called Bill. Back to the woman who plays golf and does not speak to her mother. Back to...normal. But the problem is: What is normal?

Social opinions and normality

It is widely known that in some countries of the world today, people are forcibly subjected to psychiatric treatment for dissenting from their government's policies. They are called 'sick' because they do not conform to the ideas of the majority or of the ruling elite. 'Treatment' consists of drug therapy and counselling in the attempt to make them conform — or, as the propaganda says, to 'cure' them. 'Normality' is defined as the views of the dominant group.

Probably the news-media reports of these events have left you with a sense of horror and moral outrage. But have you ever wondered about what goes on in your own country? I'm not referring to enforced psychiatric treatment for political and religious dissidents, although it is possible that your government is doing some of that too. I am referring to the trend to define 'normality' as the self of the 'natural attitude'.

You will recall from chapter 1, that this is the commonsense self. But in the last two chapters we have seen that the commonsense self is the product of social circumstances — it varies according to when and where you were born. It may be 'normal' in a communist country to report your parents' secret religious meetings to the authorities. In another country it may be just as 'normal' to report your communist parents' plans to blow up the village church. What was commonsense for Nazis was plain madness or evil in the judgment of most human beings.

It is quite inadequate to define 'normality' as the natural attitude self. It simply means that the ruling group, whether they be a democratic majority, the tyrannical few or popular opinion, decides what is normal. Because we do not share the assumptions of people living in countries with different political or religious views to our own, we easily see through their attempts to pressure people into conformity. It is much harder to see the same thing when we do it ourselves, especially if the pressure is applied with subtlety. That is why there is a growing danger in Western countries today that people like Eva will be treated by psychiatrists for asking ultimate questions. They will be thought insane because they dare to question the commonsense identity of the majority, a common sense which more and more ignores the transcendent self.

Answers to ultimate questions

It is quite silly therefore to say that people who ask ultimate questions are sick, because every one of us asks them. And we cannot say that every one of us is sick, because that leaves us with no example of a healthy person with whom to compare our own sorry state. Ultimate questions are normal; it is the *answers* that vary. But if we can convince people that our own answers are 'normal' and other people's 'sick', then we can manipulate unbelievers and make them conform to our own ideas.

We can see this in the case of Eva Adamson. Her husband and friends consider her to be sick when she starts to question the answers they take for granted. What they really want from psychiatric treatment is pressure to make Eva conform to their own answers to the ultimate questions. If they can find a psychiatrist who shares their beliefs, Eva will become subject to a whole propaganda apparatus, including the chemical manipulation of her brain. However, it may not be necessary for them to go this far; simply suggesting to Eva that she is sick may be sufficient to produce conformity.

Eva's doubts were produced by a priest. We can see how answers to ultimate questions vary, by comparing her husband and friends' answers with those of the priest. The following diagram gives two sets of answers to three ultimate questions. Those on the left (part A) are the answers of Eva's husband and friends — answers which are becoming 'common sense' in modern Western societies. Those on the right (part B) are the answers of the priest — typical of what Roman Catholic Christians believe.

Question	*Answer A*	*Answer B*
Who am I?	You are Eva Adamson, wife, mother, dinner-party live-wire and golfer.	You are Eva Adamson, a spiritual being created by the eternal God after his own likeness.
What is the purpose of my life?	To enjoy the everyday world, have a happy marriage, bring up your children well, and to get as much money and leisure time as you can.	To so be and act that you find your true fulfilment in mystical union with Almighty God.
What will happen to me when I die?	Do not think about it — just get on with everyday living.	You will journey into the divine presence for judgment. You will continue to exist forever but, depending upon the moral and spiritual state of your soul, you will either live more fully or less fully than before.

Now it is not my intention to suggest that one set of answers is true and the other false. But it is my intention to say that the proper way to deal with these answers is to ask whether they are true or false, and not whether they are normal or abnormal. To decide whether or not either set of answers is true, we would have to test them against our total experience of 'reality'. That will have to come later. All I want to do at the moment is to point out the danger of substituting a misleading medical analogy for this matter of truth and falsity. This is what allows some communist governments to foist their definitions of identity on to dissenting citizens in the name of therapy. It is what also allowed the psychiatry lecturer, of whom I spoke earlier, to dismiss Jesus Christ's sense of identity as schizoid.

By using a false analogy from physiological medicine, people are able to link the popular prestige of psychiatry and psychology with their own beliefs about identity, and define anybody who happens to disagree with them as 'sick'. This is the same kind of hocus-pocus the Church itself once used to eliminate heresy. At least a heretic had a slim chance of survival, if he could prove that his beliefs were true. But when truth does not even enter the issue, when all is either health or sickness, the only way out is conformity or 'treatment'.

This modern thought-trick can be exposed for what it is by turning the medical analogy back upon those who use it. For example the great psychologist Sigmund Freud, who more than anyone else is responsible for the use of this medical analogy, regarded people who believe in God as mentally ill.

According to Freud, they have not sufficiently grown up to be able to stand on their own two feet as mature adults — they need a parent figure. So out of their wishful needs they project the existence of a giant, protecting parent to watch over them: God.

But this argument can be used as successfully in reverse. One could say that Freud and all other atheists are suffering from a parent *death-wish* complex — that because they were never able to establish a happy relationship with their parents, they secretly wished their parents would die. But fearing the legal consequences of killing their parents whom they can see, they now fulfil the wish by killing the divine parent they cannot see.

Using the kind of evidence Freud employed to support his view, it would not be difficult to 'prove' this opposite case. But hopefully nobody would be silly enough to waste their time on such a project. The medical analogy is fallacious. We should drop it for good and start speaking again about true and false, instead of normal and abnormal identities. What we should be asking about the various answers to the ultimate questions is whether or not they fit the facts of experience, all of our experience. The problem with the commonsense answers of Western people today is that they leave out the very centre of our experience, the transcendent self.

In this chapter I have deliberately introduced the possibility of religious answers to ultimate questions, to pave the way for the next stages of our journey into the search for human identity. Throughout history it has been religion which has provided most people's answers to these questions.

But today not only is there a growing distrust of religion, but also a belief that it is quite possible to live without being religious at all — to be secular. In the next chapter we will begin to explore the nature of the transcendent self, an exploration that will lead to the conclusion that being nonreligious is impossible.

6
A hole in reality

IDENTITY AND THE TRANSCENDENT SELF

Modern physicists increasingly tend to think of the universe as great bundles of energy. To me a piece of ordinary rock looks inert, hard, like a completely dense substance. But to modern physicists that same piece of rock looks like a magic wonderland. The scientist sees in it the dance of the universe — millions of electrons whirring around millions of nuclei. For him it is more *empty* than solid — like a concentrated honeycomb. He knows that if all the energy in a large piece of rock was released at once, it would be almost enough to blow up the world.

It is hard to find appropriate mental pictures for modern physics' descriptions of matter as electrical energy or charged particles. Most of us still think in terms of 'thing' or 'substance', but words like 'power', 'forces' or 'spiritual' seem to be closer. In modern physics a piece of rock seems more like a science fiction 'reality barrier' than a thing.

This almost 'spiritual' quality of the natural universe has been extended further by what modern science has discovered about time. It now appears that if we could travel at a speed near to that of light then, as far as people who remained living normally on earth were concerned, we would live for hundreds or even thousands of years. Strange as it may seem, the idea of nearer-to-immortal beings is by no means foreign to modern science. But this almost semi-mystical quality of reality is not the way science has always pictured the universe.

The universe as a machine

Until relatively recently science mainly thought of the universe as a great big machine. The picture frequently used was that of a clock. According to this image the universe worked to regular laws set by the various interrelations of its pieces, just as a clock works by the fixed inner principles of its springs, cogs, wheels, hands etc. Nor, by the way, has modern science discarded this picture of the universe as a machine. It is still an exceedingly useful picture for trying to map that complex reality which we call the universe 'out there'.

But this particular way of thinking caused a dramatic change in the way religion came to think about God. Instead of being 'close' to the universe and to human beings, God began to be seen as a great, supernatural watchmaker. God, it was thought, made the 'clock universe', wound it up and then, apart from an occasional piece of tinkering (miracles), left it ticking according to the inner laws of its own making. Whereas religion used to think of God as being intricately involved in the universe's workings, now it thought of him as quite remote from it. He was becoming a God only of the *gaps* in human knowledge about the universe, invoked to explain what science could not explain. Every advance in scientific knowledge pushed this picture of God further back from the world of human beings. God became the mystery that was left over.

To those who realized that the mystery of the universe was infinitely greater than our scientific knowledge about it, God remained important as the final explanation of everything — but very remote. In part this explains why people who live in countries most influenced by modern science still practise religious funeral rites extensively, even though they do not normally attend services of worship or pray. God only seems real for them at the remote edges of life. But other people became sceptical about religion, thinking that what today was explained by religion would tomorrow be explained by science. They tended to forget about God altogether.

In the popular Western mind the great machine continues to be the main picture of the universe. It is the chief reason why modern people find it hard to see how God could be relevant or close to them, or why it is hard to believe in God at all. The human person, what we have been calling the transcendent self, seems to be an enigma, an alien in a machine world.

Misconceptions

Now I want to clear up two possible misconceptions which may have arisen about this transcendent self. You will recall from earlier chapters that two things have been claimed about it. First, that it is there — that there is a part of us which 'rises above' our natural and human environment. Second, that it is the clue to our real identities.

But perhaps you are thinking that the transcendent self is another 'God of the gaps'. From what has been said about it so far, it could appear to be just a minor, unexplained leftover of modern natural and social science. People may be left thinking something like this:

> *Natural science explains the origin and functioning of the human body. Social science explains how we develop a mind and a self. Surely the fact that there is a bit of mystery left over — call it personality, self-consciousness, transcendent self, or whatever — is very shaky ground on which to build a story about the real identity of human beings. It sounds like a man trying to live off the crumbs which have fallen from the dinner table. Instead of creating some explanation of identity based on this mnysterious transcendent self, wouldn't it be more sensible to wait for science to come up with an explanation of it?*

The first misconception which may have been created is exactly this impression that the transcendent self is a leftover like the God of the gaps. It is true that we have always discovered it at the end of our various journeys into identity. This may have given the false impression that it is the last and unexplained link in a long chain of explained links. But this is not the case. On the contrary, the transcendent self is the *explaining* mystery of human being, not its unexplained mystery. This can be made clearer by a practical example.

Suppose that I am standing in my garden on a summer's day, admiring the beautiful eucalyptus tree which I planted there two years ago. If I were a natural scientist, I might begin explaining to myself what is occurring in my perception of this lovely tree. I might think of the sun as a light source, beaming its rays down on to the tree and reflecting its image into my eyes. Then I might think of the activity happening in the region of my optic nerve — of the conversion of the reflected light into electrical impulses sent along the pathways of my brain. Finally I might think about the chemical and electrical changes happening inside the brain itself in response to the impulse signals.

But if I were a poet or an artist, I might try to appreciate the tree more deeply, examining its effect on me and why I found it so beautiful. I might even feel that there was some kind of message in the tree, some important experience which neither scientific language nor ordinary speech could capture. I would try to help myself clarify and understand this 'experiencing' of a tree. Finally, as an artist I might attempt to express the distillations of my feelings and responses in poetry or paint.

Now it is the self which has the ability to 'stand back', not only from the tree but also from my perceptions and feelings about the tree, which is the transcendent self. Without this self we could not form scientific explanations or artistic impressions. The transcendent self remains a mystery, but it is the explaining (scientific) and understanding (artistic) mystery of human being. It is not a leftover which we discover at the end of these creative processes; it is there all the time, doing the thinking and the understanding.

Obviously whatever it is, the transcendent self has a very close connection with nature, and especially with human biology. We noted this fact in chapter 2 where we talked about brain chemistry and brain damage. There is plenty of other evidence too. For example, biological adults more easily imagine their own death than biological children, suggesting that the development of the transcendent self grows in step with the development of the brain.

Drugs also affect its functioning. For example, hallucinogens tend to suppress or destroy its ability to discern the difference between private phantasies (inner reality) and the shared human world ('out there' reality). Other drugs, for example anaesthetics, seem to turn it off or push it deeply under.

Biological death seems either to turn it off or to send it completely away. In fact it is virtually impossible to imagine it being turned right off, because you have to use the transcendent self itself to do the imagining, thus being reminded that it is turned *on* and working. We can more easily imagine it going away somewhere else, because it is constantly doing that in its own imaginings. Indeed the ability to shift about imaginatively — to phantasize yourself as a duck or an astronaut orbiting around Mars — is one sign of possessing a transcendent self.

We also saw in chapter 3 that, in order to reach

its potential, the transcendent self needs the conversation of human relationships. Thus whatever it is in itself, we must never overlook its dependence upon the natural and social worlds which, enigmatically, it surpasses and 'rises above'.

Moreover, no amount of increased knowledge or understanding detracts from the essential *mystery* of the transcendent self. Because it is itself the instrument of human knowledge and understanding, any increase in these things only enhances our sense of both its reality and mystery. To summarize, the transcendent self has two essential qualities:
(a) it is the centre of what it means to be human, and
(b) it eludes every attempt to rationally explain it — trying to explain the transcendent self is about as futile as commanding the cart to pull the horse.

A second misconception which may have arisen is that the transcendent self is a thing or substance. When the modern science of anatomy began, some religious people thought that one day an anatomist would discover the soul. There was even speculation about its actual location within the human body; betting favoured the base of either the pituitary or pineal gland. Alas, no cry of 'Eureka!' has yet sounded from the lips of an anatomist, announcing to the world his discovery of a substance called 'soul'. There are no souls in laboratory specimen jars, on microscope slides or even, as some might expect, floating ethereally in glass gas bottles. And lest it be thought that the soul substance had already fled the anatomist's corpses, it must also be noted that no surgeon has found a soul-like thing whilst operating on a living human being.

Now it has never been intended that we should think of the transcendent self as a thing or a substance residing in the human body, however wispy or vapour-like. Later we will have to say, with as much precision and clarity as the case allows, just what the transcendent self is. But it is certainly not intended that we should think of it as any kind of object which could be discovered 'out there'. We have already seen that the transcendent self is the *person* — a knowing subject, not a known object. In fact it seems to be the cardinal virtue of every human moral system that we should never treat a person as an object.

Later we will come to understand more about the transcendent self by considering how persons relate to each other, how they come to understand each other and the kind of moral values that govern their relationships. We will also consider what the vast majority of religious people mean when they say that the soul is not a material substance at all, but a spiritual being. But for the moment we need only see that the transcendent self is not a thing in the material sense.

What is the transcendent self?

How then should we think of the transcendent self? For the time being it is probably best to think of it as a *hole* — a vacancy or emptiness. This may not be easy, because it is a strange way of thinking. An analogy might help.

When scientists talk about 'space', they mean that near vacuum, that virtual nothing, between the stars and the planets. Somehow it is nothing and something at the same time. Spaceships can travel through it and so can communication signals. That is what the transcendent self is like — no 'thing', but still very real.

Another analogy will help fill out the picture some more. We could think of the transcendent self as a kind of vacuum. To create a vacuum we have to pump all the air out of an enclosed container, until there is nothing left inside. This container must be strong enough to maintain the atmospheric gap against the pressure of the outside air, which wants to rush back inside and fill it again. The transcendent self is not an atmospheric vacuum, but a meaning and morality vacuum. There is nothing inside human beings which automatically decides what they shall live *for* and what they shall live *by*, just an emptiness. We ourselves have to choose what to fill this vacuum with. No human being is strong enough to keep this meaning-morality vacuum empty, even if it was thought desirable to do so. In practice everyone lives for something and by some kind of moral standard.

Perhaps it is still not altogether clear how one can think of the transcendent self as a hole or emptiness. As it is such an important concept, it is worthwhile looking at one last example.

Imagine a brilliant but wicked psychologist. Instead of playing around with rats in mazes, he acquires half-a-dozen tiny orphan babies. He places them in a huge steel dome, say three hundred metres in diameter and eighty metres high. They are not allowed any contact with outside human beings whatever, including the psychologist himself. Inside the dome the psychologist has contrived all the necessary requirements to allow his experimental human animals to survive for twenty years. So far as they know, there is no other world outside their dome. Perhaps as the years pass they begin to wonder if there is anything outside or whether the curved steel walls just go on forever, but they have no means of testing the theory. So far as they are concerned nothing exists except their own little social world and the things inside the dome. Meanwhile the psychologist spends his days observing life inside the dome through a one-way window hole right on its top. He can see anything his experimental subjects ever do.

Now this is what I mean by calling the transcendent self a hole. The dome represents the world we live in, natural and social. The one-way mirror in the hole on top of the dome represents the transcendent self. The transcendent self is a hole in our reality — a hole in what otherwise seems to be an enclosed universe or some kind of giant machine.

Of course, like any example, the parallels are not perfect. We know that there is a hole in our world; the experimental humans did not know that there was one in theirs. Also we are both inside our universe (like one of the experimental humans) and also the 'hole' through which we observe the universe (like the one-way mirror hole and psychologist combined). In some sense or other the transcendent self can 'get outside' our world and outside the rest of the self too. It is a reality gap.

The fear of freedom

You will recall that we discovered the transcendent self right at the beginning of this journey into human identity, when we began to ask questions about who we really are. That is to say, we discovered that there is a part of every human being — the most real and essential part — which wants to know what it is, what it is meant to be doing here and how it is meant to do it.

Whatever the answers are, if there are any at all, they are not automatically pushed on us by the nature of things — this is the human gap. As we have seen, many people try to avoid the gap altogether. It terrifies them, so they try to live as if it was not there. They decide to live in the everyday, so-called commonsense world, accepting its meaning and values as if they were eternal, unavoidable truths — or at least trying never to doubt whether they are or not. Like ostriches with their heads in the sand, they think that what you choose not to see is not really there.

But to bury your head in the sand, as every ostrich who has felt the hunter's net entangle it knows, is just as much a commitment with consequences as trying to find an escape. For human beings the escape would mean discovering some kind of authentic meaning and values, meaning and values that accorded with our whole experience of reality, including the reality of the transcendent self. But if there is one thing that the transcendent self does have to do, it is this: it has to choose what to live for and what to live by. Fooling yourself into believing that you do not have this choice is probably the most inhuman act you can perform on yourself. It is like trying to turn a person into a thing.

In the next chapter we shall see that 'religion' is the

best word to describe whatever it is that we do actually choose to live for and by, even if we have chosen to accept the so-called commonsense world. As we are already part of the way to this conclusion, it may now help to put it into the form of a simple verbal equation. It goes like this:

To be human	=	to be a trans-cendent self	=	to choose meanings and values for life	=	to possess a religion

This chapter began by examining how modern scientific knowledge tended to push traditional religion's picture of God out into the gaps in that knowledge. If we imagine that the universe is a great whirlpool then, whereas God was once pictured at its centre, the scientific knowledge explosion has made it seem as if God is just the foamy froth at the outer edges. But our exploration of the transcendent self may already be giving us solid grounds to doubt this new, remote picture of God. At first it looked as if the transcendent self was at the foamy outer edges of the human whirlpool too. But on closer examination we discovered the reverse; it was at the very centre. Could we have made the same mistake about God?

Suppose that instead of picturing God as an object, a thing 'out there' in the universe, we picture him as being like a person, a subject, a transcendent self. (In fact this is exactly how traditional Christianity has always thought of God.) Then suppose that we are asked, 'What is God's relationship to the universe like?' Now instead of replying, 'Like a watchmaker to a watch', we would reply,

'Like the relationship of a transcendent human self to nature and society'. With this picture we can easily imagine how God could be both 'above' the universe and 'close' to it at the same time, for that is exactly our own relationship to it. But this is only a beginning; we will have to come back to these matters later.

7

The hoodwinking self

IDENTITY AND RELIGION

Imagine again the scene where Eva receives a visit from her parish priest. But suppose that instead of taking the priest's questions to heart, she protests that she is not interested in religion and that she does not believe in God. But the priest is an old hand and immediately comes back with, 'Which God is it that you don't believe in Mrs Adamson? I may not believe in that God either'.

This would probably stun Eva momentarily. It has not occurred to her before that people use the name 'God' with different meanings. If she is fairly typical, Eva's picture of the God she does not believe in is likely to be quite crude. Almost certainly she will be thinking of a God who is supposed to be somewhere *up* or *out there* in the space-time universe. But Eva cannot believe in this picture of God. Eva thinks it is childish. It reminds her of the Russian cosmonaut who said he had been 'out there' and could not see God. What Eva does not realize is that her priest finds this picture childish too. Christianity has never thought of God as an object 'out there' in the space-time universe. Quite the contrary, Christian theology thinks that space and time are just part of the whole natural universe which God has made. If God is in that universe, it is only in the sense that an artist is *in* his painting, an architect is *in* his design, or an engineer is *in* his bridge.

Eva would not be unusual if she had even cruder pictures than this in her mind. I have met atheists whose rejected God was rather like a bearded superman, supposedly living somewhere between the upper atmosphere and the sun — the kind of God a preschool child might believe in. I do not know where they got such crude pictures from. Perhaps they had been taught them by some naive person who should never have been let loose on a Sunday School class! But I always think that there is a bit of dishonesty about this sort of atheism. Such people seem to find it rather convenient to disbelieve in such an unbelievable God.

But let us suppose that having failed to deter the priest with her professed atheism, and not wanting to be troubled about religion, Eva tries another tactic. She says to the priest, 'Father, I respect your beliefs, I know you're a dedicated and sincere man, but I'm not really religious myself'.

Old hand or not, this will put the priest on the spot. Now she is saying that religion is all right for those who need it, but she does not need it. There is also a gentle hint that being religious is a little odd or weak, but of course she respects religious sincerity — patronizingly. Flustering a bit, the priest responds: 'When you say that you're not religious, do you mean that you don't like church services, hymns, confession, sermons and that sort of thing?'

'Yes,' replies Eva, 'but more than that. I mean I'm not religious in any way at all. I don't resonate with religion — don't feel anything. I just don't need religion.' In other words Eva is trying to say that, just as some people are not musical or arty, she is not religious. If your ear is insensitive to tone, you cannot sing. Eva is saying that she has no religious sensitivity, and that she does not care about it either.

Now it is quite possible to lack musical or artistic sensibilities — they require a certain kind of temperament or ability. But it is impossible to be nonreligious. Mostly when people think of religion, they automatically think of one of the great world religions. This is hardly surprising: for centuries these religions have supplied the vast majority of human beings with their meanings and values. Their influence on human history has been profound. But it is a mistake to equate religion as such with any one or even all of them together. Often when people say that they are not religious, what they really mean is that they are not Christian, Muslim, Buddhist or a follower of some other great religion. But this does not have the same meaning as saying, 'I am not religious at all'.

It is a simple fact that, throughout history, most human beings have accepted some kind of traditional religious meaning and values to fill the human gap we talked about earlier. Sometimes the religion centred around a tribal or national deity, sometimes it was a pantheon of gods and sometimes one universal God. Perhaps what modern people really mean when they say they are not religious is that they do not believe in God — any kind of God. But then neither do many Buddhists, so does that mean Buddhism is not a religion? If not, what is it? Or to put the problem another way, when is a religion a religion and when is it something else? What is religion anyway?

These days it is widely believed that many people can fill their meaning-morality gaps without being religious at all. There is nothing new in this, except in the scope of it. In the past the atheist or non-religious person tended to be unusual — some kind of freak. Everyone knew what such people did not believe or practise but, because they were so few in number, no one bothered much about what they did believe or practise. Now all this has changed. In the modern world whole countries claim to be nonreligious, atheism being a basic belief of Communism. Such people, so the belief goes, fill up their human gap with Marxism instead of religion. The Western world is also supposed to be becoming increasingly nonreligious and undergoing a process of secularization. The assumption is that to be secular is to be nonreligious.

But how can we say that people are not religious if we cannot say what religion is? In the case of Western countries, it is quite true that church attendance is low, people do not pray much and religion seems to have hardly any influence on everyday life. But this is only to observe that Western people do not believe or practise traditional Christianity to the same extent as they did in the past. It is not the same as saying that Western society is more nonreligious. It could well be that secularism (whatever it is) is really a religion itself.

And is it true that Communists are not religious, or is Marxism itself a religion? There are many people, expert and nonexpert, who believe that it is. What we really need to know is just what religion is.

The meaning of religion

There are two ways to define religion. We can define it *substantively* or *functionally*. An example will help to show the difference between the two.

Imagine a primitive hunting tribe who have never eaten anything in their lives except milk and meat. Ask them to define 'food', and they reply with a description of milk and meat. For centuries 'food' in their language has had absolutely no other meaning than milk and meat (a substantive definition). But secretly one tribal hunter, sick of the endless hunting stalks, has been sneaking out into the jungle at night gathering wild berries and potato roots. Gradually he has introduced his own family to the new fare and they are thriving. If we ask these vegetarians to define 'food' they will describe not only milk and meat, but fruit and vegetables too. When the rest of the tribe learns of the new discovery, they will have to change their definition of 'food' to include fruit and vegetables. But meanwhile another tribesman has found that eggs are good to eat too, so the problem arises whether the old substantive definition is the best way to think of 'food' at all.

'Who knows,' they think, 'perhaps there are hundreds or thousands of types of food?' One intelligent young warrior suggests that in future 'food' should mean anything that serves the purpose of nourishing the human body (a functional definition). The tribal elders agree. The old definition has had it — it does not cope with the facts anymore.

Now religion can be defined substantively — that is what we have been doing for centuries. We have said that religion is this or that particular set of beliefs, morals or rituals. Substantively, Christianity has been defined as, say, belief in the Bible or the Apostles' Creed, and the ritual practice of Holy Communion or the Mass. Islam has been defined substantively as belief in the Koran and in Allah, or the practice of daily prayers intoned with one's face set towards Mecca. Or we have been more general, but still substantive, and defined religion as 'belief in some kind of God or gods'.

The problem with substantive definitions of religion, like 'food' in the above example, is that however wide you cast the net you never seem able to fit everything in. If you define religion as Muslim or Christian beliefs and rituals, then everyone who is not Muslim or Christian is not religious — which is clearly unsatisfactory. But if you define religion as 'belief in God or gods', then a lot of Buddhists and animists are not religious — nor, contrary to widespread opinion, are Marxists. Substantive definitions do not cope with the facts.

To define religion functionally, we have to know what it does. It is fairly obvious that the main function of everything that we have been used to calling 'religion', including Buddhism, is to provide people with meanings and moral values to live by. We can best understand this by using a practical example. But first we need to recall that, within the limits set by nature and their social experience, human beings have to choose between various options of what to live for and by. This is our gap — the transcendent self vacuum which we explored in the last chapter.

Now suppose that you are a married man attending a rather swinging party alone, because your wife is ill. At this party you meet an attractive, interesting woman who invites you back to her place for 'coffee'. What will you do? Your decision is a moral one, but it will depend on the meaning with which you view the circumstances. Hormonal chemistry may be driving you in a certain direction but, as we know, there is a part of the self which can 'get above' the glands and allow you to say, 'Not tonight, thank you'. Your moral gap is open; you have to fill it in with your own choice.

Now this is where your beliefs about meaning come into play. For example, if you are a Christian and you believe adultery is a sin against God, you will try hard to refuse the invitation. Or you might be a Communist whose party branch is also opposed to adultery, because it is decadent bourgeois indulgence and saps the spirit of revolutionary fervour. This will also prompt you in the direction of refusal. But your meaning gap is open; it has to be filled by your choice too. As you contemplate sensual delight with this lovely lady, you may begin to doubt whether God really exists anyway — or question whether the Party's view is not just a hangover from proletarian, sexual repression.

Of course you may not have a sophisticated meaning system like Marxism or Christianity.

Meaning may not be what God or the Party thinks of you, but what your wife would think. Thus your meaning concerns may go no further than how adultery might affect your marriage relationship. In this case you may decide that what matters is either the moral question of deceiving your wife, or simply the practical consequences of being found out. But maybe you have already filled the meaning gap in this area of your life by opting for 'open marriage', or the belief that it is always best to follow your chemistry. In which case you will probably go and have some coffee.

Please do not think that I have chosen a sexual example because I think sex is more important than other kinds of morality. The advantage of a sexual example is that most people are able to identify with it, otherwise a soldier facing the moral dilemma of killing, or a worker facing a decision whether to strike, would suit just as well. Each situation would demonstrate the need for choice and the close link between systems of meaning and morality. This need to choose is rooted in our experience of ourselves as transcendent beings. Historically, traditional religion has functioned to provide most of us with the guidance needed to make these choices.

We are now in a position to define religion functionally. Let us call religion 'a person's ultimate beliefs about meaning and about moral values'. You can see that this easily includes everything that we are used to calling religion — the traditional 'milk and meat'. But is also means that every person is religious because, however unconscious or half thought-out, in practical life every person lives for something and by some kind of moral standards. Perhaps the belief about meaning is simply 'Let us eat and drink for tomorrow we die', but even this is a meaning-belief which will shape your life in certain directions. Perhaps the moral values are just 'Me and my family first', or 'Do other people before they do you', but these are moral values, however we may judge them.

If it is true that old 'diets', for example Christianity or Hinduism, are being given up, then some kind of new diet must have replaced them — perhaps Marxism or secularism (or astrology!). But, whatever it is, it is religion. Human beings cannot live without some kind of meaning and values, anymore than they can live without food. As Jesus Christ said, 'Man does not live by bread alone' or, for that matter, by cake and cream. Some form of religion is made necessary by the very nature of human existence. As beings who transcend our environment, we have to fill our meaning and morality hole with something. To further extend the analogy between food and religion, what we should be asking is: Religiously speaking, what are people consuming today and is it as nourishing as the old diet? We all know the difference between good food and junk food. Does the same apply to religion? These questions will form the major focus of *Part Two* of this book.

Notice that I have called religion our *ultimate* meaning and moral beliefs. I mean the meaning and values that are really important to us at rock bottom, that is the things we actually live *for* and the standards we actually live *by*, at the depth of our being. In practice every human being has a hierarchy of meaning and values, a sliding scale which registers the more important against the less important. Without such a hierarchy every time we faced a choice, even the choice of whether to get up or stay in bed each morning, we would have to work out our priorities anew. We would spend most of our lives deliberating.

Most of the time we make our choices automatically, without thinking much at all, because the situation fits into the hierarchy system we have already worked out. We get out of bed because we have to go to work. That is to say, we *have* to go to work if we want to be paid and keep our jobs. In our hierarchy, being paid and avoiding the sack is ultimately more important than another few hours sleep. It is only when we are faced with new, important or marginal situations that our meaning and moral hierarchy — our 'religion' — becomes transparent to us.

Acute awareness of death is the kind of marginal situation that brings our meaning hierarchy into focus. The death of a dear one, or a personal experience of serious illness or accident, can create this awareness. Whatever its source, death's shadow will cause us to re-examine the direction of our lives. We will try to put aside things we consider trivial and live more fully for the things that matter most to us.

If you are a person who believes that death is personal extinction, then your focus of meaning will be an increased devotion to some aspect of everyday life. Everyday reality will be at the top of your hierarchy of meaning, because you do not believe there is any meaning outside or beyond it. After your brush with death, you may even get up earlier in the morning, so that you can experience 'more' of the everyday world.

Next in priority will be whatever matters most to you within everyday life. It could be spending time with family or friends, travel, psychological growth, appreciation of nature, booze, working for charity, for justice or revolution — or just having a good time while life lasts. But if you believe in a meaning outside the everyday world, in God or an existence after death, then your focus of meaning will be an increased devotion to some aspect of that reality. (Whether it is a 'reality' outside of your own head or not does not matter for the moment.) Some kind of transcendental or spiritual reality will be at the top of your hierarchy of meaning. Everyday life will be lower down, like a dress rehearsal for the real play, but not necessarily unimportant. You will give highest priority to those things which help you to 'tune in' to this transcendental reality. It may be prayer, acts of charity, meditation, worship, renouncing wealth and living among the poor, and trying to lead a blameless moral life.

We must not get bogged down in specific examples or we will miss the point. The point is that a marginal situation like death reveals to us what we really live for — ultimately. It discloses our meaning hierarchy, our religion.

Whatever we have chosen to live for will have a profound affect on the moral choices we make — the practical side of our religion. In cases of hypocrisy, a person's moral behaviour reveals what they really believe more than their words. I suppose that this is what Jesus Christ meant when he said that his true followers would be known 'by their fruits'. But even so-called secularists can be hypocrites. I have met more than one person whose professed belief was survival of the fittest — 'dog eat dog' — but in practice they have been kind and generous to a fault. Either they had weak minds or weak stomachs.

But what people really believe about life (their deep-down meanings) will show in their actions, not necessarily by a perfect symmetry between belief and behaviour — that seems to be an impossible ideal for human beings — but by an obviously sincere attempt to put beliefs into practice. So if you believe the real meaning of life lies in the arrival of the stateless, socialist society, you will work for the proletarian revolution. Killing a few capitalists may be acceptable within your moral hierarchy. If you believe that material prosperity for yourself and your family is the highest good, you will not make sacrifices to aid starving children in poor countries. But if you believe that all life is sacred, even treading on an ant may be considered a wicked sin.

What you believe about the nature of reality and its meaning will largely determine your moral behaviour. That is why Christian theologians have always said that, in the long run, it is impossible to have Christian morality without belief in the reality of the Christian God.

Perhaps the best way to discover your own moral priorities is to ask yourself: What principles would I sacrifice everything for, even life itself? For some people the answer would be political freedom, patriotism, the right of my children to live or freedom of worship. For others it would be nothing because self is all important, the top of the moral hierarchy. But whatever your answer is, *that* is your ultimate moral value — the practical side of your religion.

Religion: upside-down or right way up?

Now I think we can see why common sense mistakenly thinks religion is some kind of belief in God, gods or spiritual reality. It is because most people throughout history have chosen to put God, gods, divine commandments and spiritual rituals at the top of the hierarchy of things they lived for and by. It is the growth of meaning and moral systems which have no belief in transcendental reality — Marxism and secularism — which has caused us to rethink the meaning of the word 'religion'. In the light of our functional definition, it would be best to call traditional religion 'spiritual' or 'transcendental' religion. This kind of religion claims that the source of authentic meaning and morality lies *outside* the everyday world.

If you turn a person upside-down, they do not change into a fence post; they remain a person — an upside-down person. It is the same with religion. Just because you turn traditional religion on its head, by claiming that the everyday world is real and the transcendental world mere imagination, does not mean that you have turned religion into nonreligion. You have just turned religion upside-down — well, upside-down from the transcendentalist's point of view anyway. For traditional religion it is the everyday world which is unreal, or only real because God has made or imagined it.

Marxism turns traditional religion on its head or, as the Marxists say, turns it right way up. But despite Marx's curious claim to the contrary, Marxism is still a religion — an upside-down religion so far as transcendentalists are concerned. Because Marxists believe that there is some kind of meaning *within* the course of human history itself, it would be best to call Marxism an 'inner-worldly' religon. A true Marxist devotee will try to 'gear into' this inner historical meaning and work for its fulfilment. 'Fulfilment' is a stateless world society which, after the appropriate revolution, will produce the beginning of 'true human history' — the Marxist's historical version of heaven or nirvana.

We should accept the label 'atheist' to apply only to Marxism's denial of a supertranscendental reality, but not to its claim to be nonreligious. From the point of view of Jews and Christians, Marxism should be called an 'upside-down religion with a lean'. Christianity and Judaism also believe that human history has an inner meaning — they believe that a transcendental God is at work in our history. Of course Marxism denies this divine purpose in history; that is why Jews and Christians might call it upside-down religion with a lean.

In the light of our functional definition of religion, secularism would be best called 'worldly' religion, because it turns traditional religion right on its head. Like transcendental and inner-worldly religion, worldly religion also comes in many varieties. But it has two basic beliefs. First, that the everyday world, the space-time universe, is the only real reality; the rest is imagination and phantasy. Second, there is no need to look for meaning and morality outside the everyday world; we are our own gods, so to speak. Devotees of this religion will live for humanity, nature or themselves — whichever they choose.

If we put all this in the category of worship, then we can say that transcendentalists worship some kind of Being or state of being which transcends everyday reality. Inner-worldly religionists worship some kind of historical force. Worldly religionists worship the everyday world, including themselves.

Each of us has a choice between these religions, or some variation or combination of them. Because practical life demands that we fill our human 'gap' with some kind of meaning and morality, we do in fact choose whether we acknowledge it or not. But it is not a choice between being religious or nonreligious — that is a modern deception. It is a choice between religions.

Of course the next question is mind-boggling: Which religion is true? The complexity and terror of this question is what has led to the secularist deception — that worldly religion is not really religion at all. For transcendentalists it is religion all right, but idolatrous religion. But even transcendentalists are divided amongst themselves. Hindus say this and Christians something else again. Even if you thought that the transcendentalists were probably right about reality, how could you ever decide between them? And if you include inner-worldly and worldly religion too, the problem is paralysing. There are so many conflicting claims! Isn't it just a matter of what you were brought up to believe anyway? Perhaps it is, but these are the kind of questions we will explore in *Part Two* of this book.

For the moment it may be worth considering this: some arrows hit the bull's-eye, some just miss it, some are in the outer rings and some do not even hit the target at all. Could it not be the same with religion? Of course being alive may not be just a game, but some kind of contest — and there are no prizes for marksmen who miss the target altogether!

You can't be nonreligious

We can now see how misleading the word 'secular' is, implying that it is possible for human beings to be nonreligious. At first people tended to believe that Marxism was nonreligious too, but the rituals and devotions of Marxism eventually created suspicion that it was really a new religion.

But the term 'secular' still fools a lot of people. It has become a propaganda word, lulling people into thinking that religious questions are dead issues. There used to be a saying amongst Christians that the Devil's greatest trick was to convince you that he did not exist. The greatest trick of secularism has been its ability to fool people into thinking that it is not a religion — that it is just common sense or science. An old proverb says that 'there is nothing new under the sun'; this is certainly true for secularism.

'Secular' is just a new name for what used to be called *idolatry,* a new name for the old religions of nature and man worship. A secular person has chosen to treat the everyday world, or some part of it, as the ultimate reality — a god. The only real difference between modern worldly religion and its ancient counterparts is that the modern version tends to drop symbolic representations of its devotional objects. We have discovered that you do not need a Bacchus myth to make the oceanic feelings associated with the consumption of alcohol your most desired life experience. Nor, in order to make 'family' your highest object of devotion, do you need a clan totem to symbolize your commitment. You can live for your family as an inward, 'spiritual' commitment. Similarly, it makes little difference whether you simply live for sex as the sublime reality, or whether you represent that commitment by phallic symbols and ritual temple intercourse.

Perhaps sexual devotees are the worldly religionists who have found it most difficult to reject symbolic representations. The modern 'sexual revolution' has moved from the how-to-do-it, sexual plumbing syndrome to mystical sex, the how-to-turn-life-into-one-big-orgasm syndrome. But at least the old totems, rituals and myths made it clear that worldly religion was religion — that the choice was between religions, not between religion and nonreligion.

Sometimes people confused the symbols with the reality they were supposed to represent. But this also happens with transcendental religion — that is why some of these religions forbid or restrict the use of symbols. Because we tend to confuse symbols with reality, I have tried to explore religion minus its various symbols, myths and rituals — to explore religious devotion as commitment to some aspect of reality as real or more real than others. Hence the three categories: transcendental religion, inner-worldly religion and worldly religion. All symbols, myths and rituals aside, these are the three basic choices facing people today.

* * *

We have now come to the end of the first stage of our journey into the problem of human identity. We began by looking at ultimate questions. Then we discovered that these questions come from a part of our being which we called the transcendent self. We saw that this self has intimate connections with nature and society, but that they cannot explain it. In fact the reverse was true; the transcendent self does all the explaining. We saw how some people try to explain away the dilemma of human identity as mental illness. Then we thought about the nature of the transcendent self and called it a 'reality hole'. Finally we discovered that we have to fill this hole by our own choice, and that what we fill it with should always be called religion.

In earlier chapters I said that we would eventually discover that the transcendent self is the clue to who we really are. Some of those clues have already begun to appear. For example, we have seen that the transcendent self is subject, not object. At the least this should cause us to cease looking for its roots (if it has any) in the world of objects, the space-time reality that science studies. Instead we should be looking outside the so-called 'natural' world.

The only reality we know to be outside this 'natural' world is the transcendent self itself. It is a transcendental reality. Our bodies are part of that larger reality which we call the 'natural' world. Could it be that the transcendent self is also part of a larger reality, a transcendental world? Are there any indicators within the transcendent self of such a larger reality? In *Part Two* we shall see that there are. But we already know other transcendent beings who are part of our reality experience — other people. We must begin to ask ourselves how we come to know them, for this might help us to see whether there is a larger transcendental reality or not.

Part Two:

The terror of choice

8

The relativist merry-go-round

MENTAL VERTIGO

In Australia most children attend State-run schools. These schools teach a 'secular' curriculum, but clergy are permitted to instruct pupils of their own religious denomination for one lesson each week. I know an Anglican minister who found his introduction to this system a shattering, but illuminating experience. He had just completed his theological training and begun work as a very raw curate. His first divinity class was a group of thirteen-year-old boys. While he was explaining the outline of the course he proposed to teach, one of the boys raised his hand to ask a question. Pleased to find that there was already some interest, the young minister said enthusiastically, 'Yes lad, what's your question?'

'Sir,' the boy replied, 'if we'd all been born in India instead of Australia, wouldn't we be Hindus instead of Church of England?' I do not know what the clergyman's answer was, because he has always found it too embarrassing to say.

What can we say to such a question? Surely nothing but 'Yes, probably we would all be Hindus'. But what is the deep meaning of the question? Obviously the young boy who asked it had something like this in mind: 'Look sir, you're going to teach us that Christianity is true, but how do we know it isn't just a lot of fairy tales? I mean, after all, there are young boys in India being taught by *their* priests that something quite different is true!'

This is the dilemma of relativism. How can we know that our beliefs about life are true? How do we know they are not simply the product of a particular kind of upbringing? Would it not be pompous or just plain one-eyed to think that our culture's ways are right and another's wrong?

Cosmopolitan relativism

Relativism is a comparatively modern problem. People whose horizons never reach further than their village or town do not experience it. They are traditionally-minded; they are what they are and could never imagine being anything else. By contrast, the relativized mind changes like a chamelon, or like an actor imagining himself into the different parts he has to play. This mind can imagine why it is what it is, and just as easily imagine itself being something quite different. To the relativized mind, life is like a play: we have all learnt a part, but we can easily imagine ourselves in someone else's part.

Communist governments understand relativism, and they fear it. That is why they prevent freedom of travel and ideas. Travel or contact with foreigners might put strange thoughts into people's minds, thoughts at variance with Marxist 'truth'. Some of the modern Islamic states follow similar policies; they restrict information, limit travel and ban outside influences like books, films, even music. The message is clear: if you wish to maintain one particular way of being human (one religion), keep people from knowing about other ways. Christians have tried it too — in the historical period when the church allied itself to the state. Some Christians would probably do it again, given the opportunity.

Modern relativism is mostly a Western experience. It is in the West that 'mind expanding' experiences like mass education, the media (especially television) and cheap travel have had their main influence. It is Western or Westernized people who think of the world as a global village. And is it any wonder, when they can watch in their own living rooms everything from the courting rituals of a tribal African polygamist, to the inauguration ceremony for a United States' president, beamed instantaneously in full colour! For such people the world has truly become a global village.

How could a young schoolboy imaginatively travel like this, and still believe that his upbringing is true but everybody else's is false? His question about Hinduism and Christianity was no smart-alec remark, nor was it the product of subversive propaganda. He was simply asking a question posed by his own life experiences. In most Western countries today, children acquire a relativized consciousness as part of the process of growing up. Conspiracy theories about subversive interests undermining traditional meanings and values miss this point.

We should not be surprised to find that relativism has grown hand-in-hand with declining church attendance and Christian belief in Western countries. Nor is there any contradiction between this and the fact that opinion polls show that the vast majority of Western people still believe in God. Because people in most cultures believe in some kind of God, God 'survives' . . . by being elevated above the mere relativities of our Western upbringing. But Christian beliefs as such appear to the relativized mind as part of a particular cultural package. It is true that a certain Christian nostalgia remains. As one sophisticated lady said to me, 'I don't mind my child being taught Bible stories — that's part of our cultural heritage — but I hope she won't fall for them and get all religious'.

But nostalgia is far from belief or faith; indeed its fashionable, paternalistic air makes belief or faith all the more difficult. Christians would probably prefer a bold denial of their beliefs about reality. Moreover the God who is above cultural relativism remains as remote as the old scientific 'God of the gaps'. Traditional ways of getting in touch with him — prayer, the Bible, worship services, the sacraments — have come under the cloud of relativist suspicion.

Relativism: the edge of a precipice?

Relativism is both a blessing and a curse. It has blessed us by enlarging our freedom of choice. It has shown us that areas of life which we thought were closed to freedom are in fact open. Suppose you believe that gravity is a freedom-limiting reality structure and that jumping from an aeroplane without a parachute means certain death. But you meet a convincing character who says, 'No, gravity isn't a reality structure — it's just in your imagination. If you keep telling yourself "there's no such thing as gravity", you'll be able to jump out of a plane and float to earth like a balloon'.

So you try it, and you die. Gravity *was* a freedom-limiting reality structure.

Now sometimes we really have been mistaken about the limits to freedom. We have confused the pressure of opinion with actual reality structures. Sex is a good example. Whatever feelings we have about it, the modern feminist movement has shown that traditional sex roles are not part of an inevitable structural reality; they are culturally relative. Feminists have drawn upon cultural variety, especially comparisons with so-called primitive societies, to show that there is nothing inevitable about the role of the male as worker, provider, superior — or the female as nurturer, domestic and inferior. In some societies these roles are mixed, or even reversed. Homosexuals have used the same kind of arguments. They have challenged the claim that homosexuality is unnatural by citing examples of social groups where it is accepted as normal.

Now I am not saying that being a homosexual or a feminist is a blessing — that is a value judgment about which people will differ and from which I wish to keep clear. I am simply noting that relativism has widened the scope of choice in these matters. In fact relativism has tended to shift the whole area of private behaviour into the realm of personal freedom. Tolerance of people 'doing their own thing' has become the highest virtue. Intolerance is condemned as narrow-mindedness or manipulation.

But freedom is a two-edged sword. Even in this world, one can just as easily damn one's life as save it. It may be exhilarating to be liberated from mere conformity to the opinions or power of others, but what do you do then? A popular song of recent times had the words, 'Freedom's just a word for nothing left to lose'. The vocalist who popularized it committed suicide. When you are through with the freedom of mere rebellion, how do you find a meaning and morality based in reality?

But perhaps the song's despairing words were referring to the relativist's freedom: do whatever you like because it is impossible to find authentic meanings and values. Here freedom is mere randomness, a will-of-the-wisp, empty and vacuous. Jesus Christ taught that 'the truth shall make you free' and, when you think about it, what else could? Rebellion is not freedom; it is the other side of conformity. Randomness is not freedom; it is the trap of meaninglessness. True freedom should be called 'the ability to choose between reality and unreality, and the knowledge to know the difference'.

Relativism's curse is the feeling that the search for meaning and moral truth is an impossible goal. We should not be surprised to find a link between the relativized mentality and increasing drug addiction, both legal and illegal. When people lose hope of finding authentic meaning and values, they will turn to all kinds of mindless, irrational mysticisms, including drugs. They will also be tempted to turn their freedom over to authoritarian cults and personalities to avoid the insecurity of empty choices.

This is becoming the major problem of Western societies: Can they maintain the freedom to choose between different ways of being human, or will the terror of freedom produce new forms of authoritarianism as people grasp after security? Will we see a return to some kind of transcendental religion which is just a mask for naked power — 'the President rules by divine decree'? Or will inner-worldly religion justify totalitarian power by its interpretation of historical forces — 'the Party certifies you insane because you represent outdated interests'?

Another way of saying all this is to ask: Can the West's growing worldly religion prevent anarchy and, if it cannot, can it prevent authoritarianism? A religion which has no meaning or morality, except what people make up for themselves, sounds like a sure recipe for the rule of the most powerful — or the war of all against all. It makes one think that the writer was right who said, 'If there was no God, it would have been necessary for man to invent one'. The tragedy of Western man is that he has given up trying to find out whether God is an invention or not.

At university I had a teacher who is the only person I have ever known who really tried to take relativism seriously. 'Truth is impossible', he said. 'Everything is relative to your social circumstances and upbringing.'

He decided that it did not matter what you thought or did, so long as you chose for yourself. Freedom was randomness. To let your choices be guided by anyone else was, he claimed, a denial of freedom. 'Meaning is what you make up for yourself, morality is whatever you decide to do — that's all.'

The strange thing was that he wanted to persuade others of the *truth* of this view. Blind to this glaring self-contradiction, some rather naive students accepted his point of view. He became their adored guru, teaching them to experiment with drugs, fool with tarot cards and do whatever they felt like doing. He said that he was his own god. His devotees could not see that he was their god too — they were too busy living out their freedom phantasies. But whenever someone threatened this man physically or emotionally, he did not say, 'Don't do that — I don't like it'. What he would say was something like, 'Don't do that — it's *unfair*'. On the negative side of morality, when someone threatened to hurt him in some way, he suddenly appealed to a universal sense of right and wrong.

These incidents reveal the self-contradiction of moral relativism. They show that relativism is either the product of shallow thinking or an excuse for selfishness.

Finding a way through

It is obviously true that much of what we believe has no foundation in any reality than other people's opinions. If you grew up in a tightly knit social circle where everyone believed that drinking orange juice produced insanity, you would no doubt share the phantasy and avoid the evil juice. And no doubt if you grew up in a Hindu or Marxist family, you would have a proclivity for believing in the truth of Hinduism or Marxism. But the simple fact that we have learnt something from other people makes it neither true nor false. We learn just about everything, including mathematics. We do not doubt that one plus one equals two just because our mothers taught it to us.

Of course you can get through life without knowing anything much about mathematics. But you cannot get through life without a system of meaning and morality, a religion. Religious truth is decided the same way as any other truth. We must ask whether the meaning and morality thoughts in our minds correspond to some reality or other, or whether they are just imaginative phantasies? We must also ask: Does our religion include all reality, or does it leave out crucial matters?

Cultural relativism does not cancel truth, but it does push it down to deeper levels. We can no longer ignore the possibility that what we believe is merely the prejudices of upbringing. But that includes worldly religion too, so-called secularism. At the deeper level nothing has changed. All the ancient issues — matter or spirit, good and evil, atheism or theism, love or power, reality or phantasy — are as relevant as they ever were. But people who live and think on the plane which takes no account of their cultural conditioning will appear naive, sheltered and parochial to the relativized consciousness.

We must begin to think of meaning and morality as a pilgrim's road, and not confuse being on the right track with having 'arrived'. We must not think that having chosen the wrong track, or taken wrong tracks, that there is no right one. The fact that it is difficult to find the 'way through' does not mean that there is *no* way.

Discovering the truth about the 'natural' world is difficult too. Scientists need patience, application and creative imagination. We should not expect religious truth to be less difficult. Even for natural scientists, the 'truth' about the natural world is always a step in the right direction, rather than complete arrival. But every step in the right direction is further confirmation that there is a real road to take. In the next chapter I will try to map out the religious path being trod by disciples of worldly religion, a path which should be called a 'way out', not a 'way through'.

9

Tunnel vision

THE WORLDLY RELIGION OF SECULARISM

We have seen that the test of a religion is its ability to truthfully interpret reality for us — all of reality. Now I want to link this idea of a test with our experience of ourselves as transcendent beings, and then apply it to worldly religion — so-called secularism.

Up to now we have thought of the transcendent self as a gap, a meaning and morality hole. But this picture is too passive. It suggests that consciousness is like a concave mirror — merely giving a condensed reflection of whatever happens to pass in front of it. In fact human consciousness is almost always intentional. Like radar, it emits a signal and receives information back from the signal. Also like radar, human consciousness is almost always consciousness of something. It may be consciousness of a slice of reality we share with others and think of as 'out there' — like the family breakfast table, or the moon. Or it may be consciousness of a private 'in here' reality — like an imaginary, solid gold table, or a moon made of cheese.

In dreams, consciousness loses this 'consciousness of' quality, and we do seem to passively experience whatever passes in front of us. But that is only while we are actually dreaming. When we awake, the remembered dream is also a 'consciousness of' experience, a consciousness of the contents of the dream. So we will have to supplement our picture of the transcendent self as something negative — a hole, a 'no thing' — with some kind of positive, active picture.

In the last chapter I defined freedom as 'the ability to choose between reality and unreality, and the knowledge to know the difference'. Freedom is the essence of being human — of not being a mere automaton in a closed, stimulus-response universe. The transcendent self is the part of us which exercises this freedom. It has the job of choosing between reality and unreality, and of knowing how to discern the difference. Actively speaking, we should think of the transcendent self as a reality- or truth-tester and as a *power to will*. Before we get into the complex and important problem of choosing a religion, which we all have to do, a simple everyday example will explain what I mean by this new definition of the transcendent self.

Deceit and self-deceit

Obviously the transcendent self has limitations as a reality- or truth-tester. It can be ignorant or mistaken. The owner of an asbestos mine may not provide his employees with special breathing apparatus, because he is quite ignorant about the cancer-causing properties of asbestos fibre. A medical researcher may not discern a link between the inhalation of asbestos fibre and lung cancer simply because he made a mistake in calculating the statistical evidence. The choice between reality and unreality does not present itself until there is some kind of *knowledge*.

But even then, the transcendent self has the 'power to will' unreality as reality or vice versa. For example, when later research shows a highly probable or definite link between inhalation of the fibre and cancer, a choice does exist. But a mine owner who unreasonably refuses to accept the evidence can be accused of choosing unreality. Moreover he will be guilty of deliberate self-deceit and immoral behaviour, putting his own greed for profits above the cost of protecting his employees' health. Another possibility is that the owner will persuade the medical researchers, in return for certain 'favours', to falsify their evidence, thus deceiving the employees about the real danger. In this case the owner and the researchers have colluded together (collective 'power to will') to deceive others about the difference between reality and unreality. Of course the mine owner may accept the truth of the new knowledge and choose to provide protective apparatus for his workers (individual 'power to will').

This example shows us several things about the abilities and limitations of the transcendent self. It shows it is possible to be either ignorant or mistaken about reality and unreality. It also shows that it is possible to wilfully deceive oneself about the difference between reality and unreality. (This is so common that it is hard to imagine how anybody could ever think right knowledge automatically produces right behaviour, yet this is a popular belief.) The example also shows that people can collude to deceive others about what is real and what is unreal.

The transcendent self and worldly religion

Now let us apply this enlarged understanding of the transcendent self to worldly religion, so-called secularism. Worldly religion tends to accept only one reality as a true reality, the world of everyday life. It is also growing fastest in those countries (mainly Western) which have been subject to the relativizing influences we looked at in the last chapter. This is not accidental; worldly religion is a response to relativism. When you become aware that people tend to believe in the religion they have been brought up to — Hindu, Christian, Marxist etc. — you start to doubt your own traditional beliefs. The easy solution is to believe only what most people seem to agree about, the reality of the world of everyday life. This world seems real not because science has proved it, as some dreary minds keep suggesting to us, but because we experience it as a *shared* world. Remember my wife's dream about my purchasing a new suit? She could not decide whether it was 'real' until she could check with me whether it happened or whether she dreamt it.

Strictly speaking we should call the world of everyday life 'the shared world of the wide-awake adult'. I say 'wide-awake', because it is possible to be in an in-between world, half shared and half not. At the breakfast table one can easily ask another member of the family something like, 'Would you pass the flying saucer, please?' instead of 'Would you pass the sugar bowl, please?' The half-awake self produced the first part of the request; the half-asleep self the second.

'Adult' is added to 'wide-awake' because children are often unclear about what realities are shared and what are not. For example, small children cannot distinguish between a parent's absence from home and a parent's death, a distinction all to clear in the shared world of wide-awake adults.

The nature of secularism

Now modern worldly religion is not simply a revival of old-fashioned materialism. An elementary recognition of this distinction probably lies behind the popular use of the term 'secular' to describe worldly religion. Old-fashioned materialism believed in the eternity of the material world. It believed that human self-consciousness (the transcendent self) was a mere offshoot of matter, an ephemeral froth produced by the efflux of matter over time. We looked at this despairing view of life, the cosmic hiccup theory, in an earlier chapter.

Materialism or, to give it a more correct title, 'the religion of matter' draws on two persuasive elements of human experience. First the fact that we did not create matter; it was here before we were born. Second that, although we can reshape and in small degree control it, matter finally defeats us through the decay and death of our own material bodies. We would like to gain victory over matter's apparent destruction of personality, but we cannot.

Nothing can alter the despairing conclusions of the religion of matter unless there is some kind of nonhuman person who can control matter better than we can. But even superior control would not be enough for, if that person is finally dependent upon matter, he will be destroyed in the end too. If there is such a person, a kind of supertranscending transcendent self, we would need to root ourselves in it to avoid our own personal destruction.

Modern worldly religion is not a revival of the religion of matter. For the disciples of worldly religion, the religion of matter is just one competing view among a number of other religious views: Marxism, Hinduism, Christianity etc. It is part of that confusing relativist swirl which produces worldly religion. Worldly religion's disciples try to avoid this giddy confusion by settling for the most obvious reality, the world of everyday life. Old-fashioned materialism tended to grow hand-in-hand with the development of modern science, stemming (as we saw earlier) from an over-emphasis on the 'out there' world at the expense of the knowing person.

Science has not caused the growth of the newer worldly religion, but it has indirectly aided it. Worldly religion is only growing in those parts of the world where science and technology have made the world of everyday life relatively safe for human beings — where, for example, most people can expect good health, adequate food, a low incidence of infant mortality and a normal life-span of seventy years or so. This allows people to adopt a state of mind where the world of everyday life is not only viewed as the sole reality, but also as ordinary reality.

Worldly religionists are people who have ceased to wonder. This is a necessary condition for continued belief in worldly religion. They must view the everyday world as ordinary, as a reality you simply take for granted. Hence the everyday world must be relatively safe and secure. Also all ultimate questions must be suppressed and experiences which produce them avoided or forgotten. You must never wonder, for example, why there is a something called 'everyday life' and not some other kind of something or nothing. You must also eliminate from your consciousness actual and undeniable experiences which might throw doubt upon faith in the everyday world as the ordinary and only reality. Dreams are a good example.

Despite the fact that we all dream several times each night, worldly religionists tend to ignore dreams completely. Most of the (Western) followers of this religion cannot even remember their dreams. Some of them have done this so successfully that they think they do not dream at all. There is no sense, as with some other religions, that dreams might be another reality, or a channel into another reality. In fact there is no sense of dreams at all; worldly religionists just ignore dream reality. To take any account of dreams would produce wonder about everyday-life consciousness, and worldly religion cannot afford to allow wonder. It must maintain the sense of ordinariness at all costs.

Now I do not want to question the reality of the world of everyday life. I too get up in the morning, talk to my family, greet the postman, read the newspaper and participate in the thousand and one other experiences which confirm the reality of that particular world. What I do want to question, seriously and deeply question, is the wisdom of treating this particular world as the ordinary and only true reality. People who do this are playing a game, a dangerous game of phantasy.

Secularism as a game

I wonder if you have ever thought what happens when we play games? Most of us like games, but we probably could not say why. Some of us like vigorous games like tennis or football; others like quieter games like billiards or cards. But why do we like games? The reason is because we delight in the magic phantasy we create in order to make a game a game.

Earlier in this chapter we saw that the transcendent self was both our reality- or truth-tester, and our 'power to will'. And as we saw in the case of the asbestos-mine owner, we can use our 'power to will' to deceive ourselves about the difference between reality and unreality. In an ordinary game, say tennis or cards, we use our 'power to will' in order to create a phantasy world, the world of games. But we know the difference between the world of the game, a play world, and the world of everyday life, a work and responsibility world. We make up phantasy worlds ourselves. Reality worlds are just there.

We have seen that one way to test the difference between a reality and a phantasy world is to discover whether or not we share it with others. But phantasy worlds can be shared too. Games are shared phantasy worlds, common worlds of make-believe. But there is another test too. Reality always has a resistant quality. You cannot wish it away, and you cannot wish it into being what you want it to be. By contrast phantasy is always pliable; you *can* wish it away and you can wish it into being what you want it to be. In phantasy a selfish, boring man might be a great lover, but in reality the only women he ever has are the ones he pays to have. Magic and superstition entirely depend on people being duped about the difference between reality and phantasy. But of course most of the duped are self-duped because, if you believe a thing to be real, it will be real in its consequences, whether or not it is real in fact.

Worldly religionists try to use their power to will in order to treat everyday life as a game. But to do so they must deceive themselves; they must confuse phantasy and reality. They must not only play at pretending, but also keep themselves from knowing that they are only pretending. We can see how this works by thinking about worldly religion in the light of the three main elements in the magic world of play. We shall also see that worldly religion's game points away from itself to deeper-down realities behind the everyday world.

(a) The suspension of reality

Players have to agree that nothing really matters in their game world — no dire consequences hinge on the outcome. By convention the game is a phantasy enclave, a world set apart from ordinary life. For the duration of a game, reality is suspended. Here there are no worries about earning a living, making ends meet, coping with kids; no murders, no famines, no earthquakes, no death. The game's magic is destroyed as soon as anyone introduces serious consequences to it — like being angry for losing, or playing for stakes that really do matter. That is why professional games cease to be games for those who play them, although they may remain games for spectators. In the world of the game everything always turns out all right; nothing really hurtful or destructive can happen to you.

Now worldly religion pretends that this is true or ordinary life too. Of course I do not mean that worldly religionists are stupidly blind about all the things that can go wrong in a person's life. I mean that they *pretend* that everything will be all right in the end. Because modern science and technology have made the world of everyday life relatively safe, worldly religionists can go through most of life believing this phantasy and ignoring any indicators to the contrary. It is a phantasy because they have no grounds for believing it, except wishful thinking. Let us imagine a typical scene where this wishful spell is cast.

Imagine an ordinary house, with the family quietly asleep in the early hours of the morning. Suddenly the calm is rent by a child's piercing scream. The child's mother immediately wakens and rushes to his bedroom. 'What's up darling? What's all the fuss about?' she asks.

For a moment the child's shrieks continue. The mother realizes he has been having a nightmare. She draws him half out of the bedclothes and into her arms. 'There, there', she says softly, stroking his forehead.

Between sobs and gulps the little boy begins to tell his mother about the nightmare. A monster had been chasing him and, just as its horrid claws were about to close around him, he tripped and fell . . . and fell . . . and fell. There was nothing to land on. Telling the story causes the sobbing to start again.

'It is all right, all right', his mother assures him.

She reaches out and switches on the bedside light. A soft warm glow fills the room, bringing to clear outline its familiar contours — the boy's wardrobe, his little play desk, his teddy bear. 'See,' says the mother, 'everything is all right. There are no monsters — just teddy. Everything is all right'.

This is a scene familiar to every household with children in it. But is the mother lying to the child? Do all mothers and fathers lie when they so assure their children that everything is 'all right'? How do we know that everything is all right? Could it be that the nightmare is real, or an insight into the real condition of human beings? Could the child's dream be a kind of prophetic experience of matter and time, dragging his personality and self-consciousness relentlessly down into the pit of nothingness? Believers in the religion of matter would probably think it was. Or could the dream be a pale reflection of the Devil and hell — of a real monster that really does want to devour us, of a real experience of forever fading but never fading away?

A lot of believers in transcendental religion would not dismiss this possibility lightly. But worldly religionists do not believe in dreams. They say dreams are unreal — and perhaps they are. But neither do worldly religionists believe that our lives may end in dire consequences — in nothingness or hell. They cannot say why. In fact they would rather not think about this subject at all. They live *as if* God was in his heaven and all is right with the world, but they do not really know if they believe in God or not. Everything is all right, they say — and tell their children!

(b) A consensus about rules

A strictly agreed set of rules is the second important element of the magic world of play. The rules must apply equally to every participant. If there is an umpire or referee, he must show no special favours. Disputes are easily settled by reference to the rules. The game's magic is destroyed if someone cheats, or if there is a serious disagreement about interpreting the rules. Unless every player believes that the rules apply to themselves as well as others, this game world will soon dissolve. There must be commitment to the phantasized 'right and wrong' laid out in the rules.

Worldly religionists pretend that moral rules really apply to everyday life too. Amongst its followers you will never hear a parent say to a child, 'Do not do this because I have invented a rule which says it is wrong to do it', or 'You must behave this way because society and tradition say so'. Of course all sensible worldly religionists, like all other sensible people, know that many rules are just made up by parents, by people acting together (society), or by our forbears (tradition). But worldly religion's disciples do not believe that all right and wrong is merely human invention. They teach morality to their children *as if* it was part of the structure of reality itself.

As one might expect, the children of worldly religionists are becoming increasingly suspicious that the morality they are being taught is just human invention, just Mum and Dad's blind acceptance of social convention and tradition. This suspicion is likely to increase, because worldly religion has no reason for its beliefs about right and wrong.

Like everyone else, worldly religionists fail to keep the rules they teach. But, when they break a rule, they do not call it a sin against God or disloyalty to the Revolution. They tend to excuse their own misdemeanours as mistakes, or by claiming that the rule was only a human invention anyway. But when someone is about to wrong them, it is a different story! They appeal to a universal sense of right and wrong, with all sorts of talk about justice and fair play.

If you find this difficult to believe, then just try cheating your most secular of secular acquaintances and you will find that he/she will moralize as vehemently as a puritan in a brothel, but without as much rational cause. Worldly religionists act as if morality was a structural reality transcending mere human invention, but they tend to be vague about the roots and sources of such reality. As usual they would rather not think about the problem at all. They like to think that everything is not permissible, as if there really is a great umpire of human behaviour — well, their children's and other people's behaviour anyway!

(c) The transformation of time

Of all the elements in the magic world of play perhaps the most enchanting is the transformation of time. Time does not matter in this world; it stands still. There is no such thing as time in a game: no bus to catch, no deadline to meet, no work to be done. The duration of a game is the eternal present. You can catch a sense of the timelessness of games by watching children at play or, better still, by trying to call them out of the time-spell for dinner or a bath. As soon as we are worried about time, about things we have to do or places we have to be, the magic spell of the game gets broken again. That is why we try to play on a holiday or a weekend — to keep time from intruding into our play.

Worldly religion pretends that the world of everyday life is timeless too. In secular societies youth is idolized and knowledge preferred to wisdom or age. Disciples make great efforts to remain young: dying their hair, having facelifts, wearing toupees, consuming vitamins and aphrodisiacs. They will refer to someone as middle-aged not when they reach thirty-five, but fifty-five or even sixty. People who talk about death are dismissed as morbid. And worldly religion has developed new funeral rites. No longer do families prepare the bodies of their own deceased for burial or cremation. Bodies, still warm, are whisked out of the house by hired professionals, even in the middle of the night. The bereaved are sedated with drugs lest the reality of death disturb the ordinariness of the everyday world. In every possible way worldly religion suppresses awareness of death. Its disciples try to live as if everyday life was eternal. So successful is this endeavour that people living in countries permeated by worldly religion may never see a dead human body until they have nearly reached old-age themselves. Its followers live as if eternal life was not only real, but had already arrived.

The root of secularism

Worldly religion is an *as if* religion, a religion whose disciples wear reality blinkers like shying horses afraid to see anything except the world in front of their own noses. The root of worldly religion is fear. Faced with the relativist dilemma it chooses a 'way out' — into the irrational mysticism of the world of everyday life as the only and ordinary reality.

What interests me most about secular religion is not what it does see, but what it does not see. In an earlier chapter we noted that over-concentration on the world of objects, the 'out there' world, left personal life lost and alien in an impersonal universe — like a tree without roots. I suggested that, just as our bodies have their being as part of the 'out there' world, it may be that personal life has its being, not in nothing, but as part of a larger transcendental reality. But if this is true, we might expect the transcendent self to have at least some clues about its real roots. Some tell-tale clues appear in the very way secularists project their lives on to the everyday world, but they choose to ignore them.

Worldly religion shows that even when people doubt or remain apathetic towards the possibility of a larger transcendental reality, they still live *as if* there is such a reality. Now if you are dying of thirst in the desert, merely pretending that you have a well of water in front of you will not save you. But in order to phantasize the water, you need to have some idea of the reality that would actually save you.

If the everyday life of personal transcendent beings is so constituted that, in order to live it, they must act as if there is a larger reality of personal meaning and morality, then this surely suggests that they actually have some kind of experience of that reality. Disciples of transcendental religion believe that, deep down, everyone really knows that there is a supertranscendental reality, but somehow we have been cut off from close contact with it. Worldly religion seems to bear this out — with its blind, but genuine hope that everything is really all right, that right and wrong are structural realities and that we will not cease to exist.

Perhaps this sedimentary faith is a kind of genetic racial memory of the transcendental origins of personal life, or even some pale reflection of the larger transcendental reality itself. This view makes more sense that the materialist's cosmic hiccup theory, which suffers the immense difficulty of trying to explain how an impersonal universe can throw up personal, self-conscious beings. The transcendentalist's idea that we have lost touch with the roots of personal being seems to fit the facts of experience better than a theory which says that a part of the material universe has become something that it is not. The latter would be more like a miracle than an accident. Unless worldly religionists cease merely fiddling with the windlass and bucket at the top of personal being's well and draw down into that well for water, they will all die of thirst.

At the moment worldly religion mainly exists in countries where science and technology have made everyday life relatively secure, and where for centuries Christianity has been the traditional religion. Secularists try to live as if Christian meaning and morality is true, but without any commitment to the reality of Jesus Christ's God. But, we saw in an earlier chapter, Christian theology has always insisted that Christian meaning and morality cannot be maintained for long without belief in the reality of the Christian God. We can sympathize with the relativist dilemma which has produced the secular phantasy religion but, if the theologians are right, it cannot last for long.

Secularism as idolatry

Hard as it may seem, Christianity itself must condemn worldly religion as a revival of pagan idolatry. It is a case, as the great theologian St Paul would say, of 'worshipping and serving the creature rather than the Creator'. Without symbolic representation, worldly religion does indeed worship (i.e. 'give ultimate worth to') the world of everyday life. If the God of Jesus is real and not just an *as if* phantasy, then worldly religionists cannot expect to remain unscathed from their willed snub of the divine Being. But this is a theological matter which we will look at in *Part Three*.

Worldly religionists, faced with the dilemma of relativism, have decided that theology is a much too difficult subject. However this has not stopped them from creating their own superficial theological phantasy. In the face of the breakdown in meaning and moral values likely to follow in the wake of this pretend religion, we may find that the difficult has become absolutely necessary.

The ancients believed that placing phantasized limitations upon the richness of reality was a very dangerous procedure. They said that whenever you allowed one part of personality or reality to dominate or exclude all the other parts, you became demonically possessed. And they thought demon possession produced insanity and self-destruction.

Now nothing amuses secularists more than talk about demonic possession. With their usual penchant for trivializing human experience, secularists have caricatured demonic possession as the invasion of our bodies by supposedly fork-tailed, pointed-eared, pitch-fork-carrying devils. But, to guard against the danger of secular religion's one-dimensional reality, we will have to go beyond mere pantomime demonics.

By excluding the journey into the depths and roots of meaning and morality, secular religion is beginning to unleash powers of violence, lust and meaninglessness into those societies where it is gaining disciples. Most of its disciples do not want such powers to break out, but they cannot see that their own religion, 'neutrally' called secularism, contains these seeds within it. Blinkering its vision from the hints that personal meaning and morality is grounded in a more real reality than the world of everyday life, secularism abdicates any deep ability to distinguish between truth and error, good and evil. That is why it gradually becomes powerless to resist claims of intolerance. *Everything* must be tolerated: greed, superstition, family breakdown. Boredom and lust for power will become the bane of secularism.

When the journeying has been taken out of the mystery of being human and replaced by diversionary play-things like sensuality, consumerism and the aesthetics of television, people will soon be bored silly. They will turn to the escapist chemical-mysticisms of alcohol and drugs, or seek to renew the human journey by finding a religion more real than secularism — unless, of course, the combination of secularist apathy with secularist boredom and meaninglessness, allows power-seekers to impose their will upon human lives made trivial and insecure by secular religion. With no real ability to distinguish between good and evil, worldly religion remains highly susceptible to the creeping canker of the conscienceless rule of the most powerful.

* * *

This chapter began by widening our picture of the transcendent self. We saw that we had to think of it in more positive terms — as a truth- or reality-tester and a 'power to will'. In an earlier chapter we saw that the transcendent self is not a thing, not even a wispy, vaporous thing. Now that we have added positivity to our picture of its being, it is probably best to call the transcendent self 'spirit' or 'spiritual personality'. This traditional terminology, minus the semi-materialistic associations it has accrued in recent times, seems the best way to describe what we have discovered about it. To put it in a nutshell, we might say that the transcendent self is a non-material, personal centre of consciousness and will.

Transcendental religion claims that our real identities lie in some kind of reunion with a transcendent reality much larger than ourselves. In this chapter we have seen that there are definite hints of such a reality within human experience. But before we begin our journey into transcendental religion, we must briefly look at the other modern alternative to secularism, the Marxist version of inner-worldly religion.

10

The religion where no one looks on

MARXISM

In an earlier chapter I suggested we might compare religion with archery, in an attempt to decide which religion is true or most true. Using this analogy, each religion would be an arrow and reality itself the target. The closer a religion got to helping us find a real identity, the closer it would be to the bull's-eye. We might expect one religion to hit or get very close to the centre of the bull's-eye, another to be in the first circle, another in the second and so on, until some religions start missing the target altogether. This analogy avoids the over-simplistic belief that one religion alone is true and the rest false. It also avoids the popular but irrational belief that all religions are basically the same.

Now I have no intention of trying to explore every religion human beings have ever followed. History is littered with the corpses of failed and faded religions. I am only interested in those religions which are living options for people today. If we stick to the main outlines of these religions, the task of finding a way through the complexity is not so difficult as some people make out. I sometimes think there are people who like to make religion more complex than it is, because they like to live in their own little phantasy worlds. We have already seen that the main religious options in the modern world can be reduced to three types: worldly, inner-worldly and transcendental.

In the last chapter we looked at worldly religion, so-called secularism. Using the archery analogy, we might say that of all the living religious options, secularism is probably the only one that does not hit the target at all. In fact secularism does not even bother to take aim — it simply takes no interest in the ultimate nature of reality or the ultimate identity of human beings. Like cargo cults or any other religion based primarily in phantasy, we can expect secularism to be short-lived — to be engulfed by a religion offering more reality. In this chapter we will take a brief journey into the Marxist, inner-worldly religion, popularly considered by Western secularists to be their greatest potential enemy. And if depth of reality is to be the judge, Western secularists have much to fear from the religion of Marxism.

It will be obvious from the previous chapter that I believe only some form of transcendental religion can get near to giving a satisfactory explanation of who we really are and why we are here. Thus it may seem strange at this stage of our journey to take an excursion into a militantly antitranscendental religion. But Marxism is actually a kind of crossroad between worldly and transcendental religion.

Marxism began as a criticism of transcendental religion — a penetrating and, in many ways, a true and necessary criticism. Just as it is possible to create demonic distortion by excluding all reality except the everyday world, so it is also possible to demonically exclude everything except the transcendental. Marxism came as a timely reminder that human beings have bodies, that they eat and work, that they live in society and history.

When Jesus Christ said that 'Man does not live by bread alone', he never intended us to think that man does not live by bread at all. We can only appreciate Marxist religion when we see it as a reaction to transcendental religion which was becoming demonically obsessed with spiritual salvation and which was beginning to ignore empty bellies, exploitation of labour and other social and terrestrial evils. Like all reactions, Marxism itself becomes a distortion of reality, but we must not allow this to be an excuse for ignoring its deep truths as a religion.

Karl Marx himself would be horrified, perhaps *angry* would be a more appropriate word, to think that anyone would ever call Marxism a religion. But I have met many of his modern disciples who are quite happy to accept 'religion' as an apt description of their beliefs. Marx lived in the days of scientific optimism. He sincerely believed that all his ideas were 'scientific', and many of them are very fine social science indeed. But in its totality Marxism *is* a religion — a system of meaning and morality so comprehensive that almost any and every life experience can be made to fit into it, in one way or another.

Much misunderstanding surrounds Marx's famous statement that religion 'is the opium of the people'. Marx used the word 'religion' with its traditional meaning of transcendental religion. But in the very same breath he also said that 'religion is the sigh of the oppressed creature, the heart of a heartless world'. For Marx, transcendental religion was both a very great truth and a very great illusion. In giving expression to real human suffering, he believed transcendental religion contained an enormous truth — 'the sigh of the oppressed creature'. But in turning human beings away from the material and social causes of that suffering to hopes of heaven or nirvana, Marx believed this religion was a lie — 'the opium of the people'.

Marx, and I think most people today would probably agree with him, despised that form of religion which the rich and comfortable used to justify the sufferings of the socially oppressed, and which bought off the latter's potential for rebellion by pious hopes for a better life in another world. It is more than bitter irony that Marxism itself tends to become just such an instrument of oppression.

In the Germany of Marx's youth, Christianity was becoming obsessed with the spiritual at the expense of the everyday world. Under the influence of the philosopher Hegel, the religion of the Nazarene carpenter was being turned into a set of lofty intellectual ideas. This was happening at the very time when Europe was beginning to feel the effects of the industrial revolution, a revolution which was driving peasant families from the countryside to a life of poverty, squalor and soul-destroying work in the cities. Hegel's philosophized Christianity did not provide criticism, but justification of these new evils. With Hegel, Christianity became a kind of historical fatalism: whatever is, is the will of the Absolute Spirit (Hegel's name for God).

Only against this background can we sympathetically understand Marx's religious reaction, a reaction which caused him to reject a religion of mere ideas and interpretation of reality. 'The philosophers', Marx said, 'have only interpreted the world . . . The point, however, is to change it'. With this revolutionary cry Marx hoped to redress the injustices of capitalism and the industrial revolution. Hegel with his philosophized Christianity would not have agreed. One might ponder where the homeless Nazarene, who taught his disciples to pray 'Thy will be done on earth as it is in heaven', would have stood. But Marx saw Christianity as the religion of heaven without earth, and so heaven became the first enemy to be eliminated. Unless, he believed, people could be turned from illusory salvation, they would not rise up and seek their salvation on earth in the form of social revolution.

A religion in touch with life

The religion of Marxism contains at least three great truths about the reality human beings experience. First is the recognition that history is fundamental for understanding the 'meaning' of human life. Marxists believe that in a very real sense human beings make themselves — not individually, but socially and historically. They express it in the saying 'history makes man; man makes history'. We saw the truth of this belief in earlier chapters, when we compared the monkey boy's life with Eva Adamson's. Human being is historical being; to be human is to be made human in a human society.

But Marxism adds another depth to this truth, a depth which has influenced every one of us to a far greater extent than we probably realize. Before Karl Marx, most history was the history of great people and politics. It was the history of kings, bishops, prime ministers, treaties and acts of parliament. But Marx saw that history is far more influenced by economics, by invention and technology, and by the social means of economic production, distribution and exchange. I only have to think of the history of my own country to realize the truth of this discovery. Australia's dependence on the production of wool and minerals for the world market has had an influence on her character and development far greater than the personality of any prime minister or any act passed by her federal parliament.

Marxism's second great truth is the revelation that many of our revered political, religious and moral beliefs are no more than rationalizations to justify inequalities in human society. This is the nub of Marx's objection to transcendental religion, but it applies much more widely. We only have to hear a rich man extolling the virtues of free enterprise — or a poor man singing the praise of socialism — to realize that each of us tends to believe in the system which will best serve our own interests. Most people do not really care whether they get the best political and economic system, just the one which most benefits them. We see the application of the same principle when minority white races justify even the most appalling black suffering on the grounds of the latter's supposed mental inferiority or as God's judgment upon their sins. Marxism exposes the depth of selfish group interest behind even the most noble-sounding morality, politics and religion.

The right of every human being to have access to the basic political, material and economic conditions which allow a life of dignity and personal fulfilment is the third great truth of Marxism. Marxists would not usually express it in such ethical language, but this is what they mean.

In the light of such lofty ideals, we might wonder why Marxism seems to go so wrong in practice? Of course there is nothing unusual in this — Jesus Christ taught admirable ideals, but in practice the Church he founded tends to become an instrument of tyranny and oppression. In fact the same is true of all religions. It would be an act of mere bias to compare the worst practice of one religion with the best of another. What we must do instead is to discover whether a religion can justifiably explain its practical failure, whether the seeds of such failure are built into some inadequacy in the religion itself and what hope it has of being able to purify itself. Although we cannot thereby excuse its practical failures, Christianity has an explanation of them which is fundamental to its beliefs: that human beings, including Christians themselves, are at root selfish and aggressive (*sinful* is the traditional word). Marxism can only explain its practical failures by claiming that the right social conditions have not yet arrived — the system is still imperfect.

But one wonders how, if all systems are merely

human creations as Marxism claims, any of them ever went wrong in the first place. Christianity believes that there are evil systems, but it also believes that evil resides within individual human beings, a belief denied by Marxism. Marxism claims to be scientific, but there could be nothing less 'scientific' than this denial of the basic selfishness and aggression of the human heart. All history and every newspaper is witness to the opposite truth.

By denying the reality of transcendental being, Marxism has made human being the measure of itself. That is why most Marxists do not like to talk about morality or ethics, but prefer instead to cloak such talk with the over-hallowed robes of 'science'. For Marxism evil does not reside in an evil will, but is merely a fault of the system — an impersonal, mechanical sense of evil. This belief is built into the religion, but if flies in the face of everything we know about human beings.

Marxists themselves are a living proof of the opposite truth. When in power they are just as evil as the people they have replaced — some would say more so! We have already seen that this belief is contradictory. If the system is evil, and human beings make the system, then human beings must be evil in the first place. To deny this is not only illogical but dangerous. Marxism has to deny it, otherwise it would have to admit to the reality of some kind of transcendental sense of right and wrong. The denial is dangerous because it rules out any external judgment of human behaviour. No one looks on in moral judgment; human beings become their own gods. If the human will is basically selfish and aggressive, and there is absolutely no reason to believe otherwise, Marxism must always tend towards the conscienceless rule of naked power and totalitarianism. The practical failure of Marxism stems directly from its inadequate beliefs about the nature of morality and the human potential for evil.

Source of strength

The strength of Marxism lies in three directions. First, and rather paradoxically, in its moral conscience, especially its concern for the exploited and downtrodden peoples of the earth. But this has no reality basis in Marxism itself. Rightly I think, it has been attributed to Marx's own Judaeo-Christian background. Marx claimed that all his views were scientific, but science can never supply moral values.

Now either moral right and wrong is a human invention or it has a source in some kind of transcendental reality. Marxism is quick to explain the morality of others as rationalized self-interest posing as truth, but it does not see itself in the same light. Nor will Marxism attribute its own morality to a transcendental source. It is this moral contradiction which eventually turns Marxism into an antihuman force. The oppression of individual freedom in Marxist countries is not an accidental flaw; it stems from the religion's failure to provide a real basis for personal morality. Once it has used naked power to implement its original but externally derived moral concerns, Marxism will go on using power because the Marxist rulers have no one to answer to except themselves. What Marxism needs, if it is to be able to purify itself, is a sense of personal sin, but its denial of transcendental reality rules out this possibility.

The second strength is Marxism's ability to explain the complex socio-economic, structural sources of injustice. There is nothing religious about this — it is just good social science. Many of the other religions, especially modern Christianity, have already begun to incorporate this part of Marxism into their own moral understanding.

The third strength of Marxism is the meaning it gives to the lives of its disciples through its interpretation of history. For this religion, history's inner meaning lies in an evolutionary clash between economic classes. It is believed that this clash will culminate in the victory of the suffering proletariat after an Armageddon-like war with capitalism. Arising from the ashes of this conflict, a new humanity will live a life of unspecified, apocalyptic bliss in a stateless, socialist society. The true Marxist devotee will 'tune in' to the historical forces bearing the seeds of revolution and become a part of them. This sense of participating in a great pattern of meaning helps to create the fervour and devotion of Marxists, even to the point of martyrdom.

I have deliberately inserted traditional religious language into the description of Marxism's interpretation of history, to draw out its similarities with Christianity and Judaism. Christians, Jews and Marxists all agree on the importance of history for understanding the meaning of human life, but only Marxists believe that it is *all* important. For Christians and Jews, history is not only the arena of man and matter, but also of God. In both these religions, God is not only in history, but also outside it. God *is* before history begins, and God still *is* after history has ended.

Marxism is not a crude materialistic religion, where everything is reduced to and determined by mere atoms and chemicals. Marxists believe in the human transcendent self; they see reality as a complex interplay between matter, history and personal self-consciousness. This is a much richer interpretation of reality than the crudities of either the religion of matter or worldly religion (secularism).

But in the final analysis Marxism breaks down into an inadequate materialism; the personal, transcendent self is doomed to nonexistence by the death of the body. Marxists will not concede that as well as being part of history and nature, we also participate in some kind of transcendental reality. Consequently Marxism has absolutely no explanation for the emergence of personal, self-conscious life in an otherwise impersonal universe — except the tricky playing with words referred to in an earlier chapter (see the note at the end of chapter 4). This despairing conclusion to life somewhat dulls the light of Marxist meaning. All those who die before the arrival of the stateless utopia never participate in their true fulfilment. There is no sense, as with Christianity and Judaism, that each human being is equidistant from his/her fulfilment in God, or that history has a purpose both within and outside itself.

This is not only a difference about irrelevant pie in the sky when you die, as Marxism says, but also a difference about how to live one's life now. As we have seen, Marxism's belief in human equality is a sentimental hangover from transcendental religion (or an unconscious awareness of transcendental morality). But if each one of us is made by the same Being, loved equally by that same Being and eventually judged impartially by that Being, the brotherhood and sisterhood of humanity has a basis in reality and not mere sentiment. It is worth noting, too, that survival after death is hardly irrelevant for human beings, although it must be called evil when it becomes an excuse for ignoring real human suffering.

Looking back over this chapter I realize that it has acquired the serious, sombre tone which I wanted to avoid. Perhaps the fault is mine, but perhaps it is because Marxism itself is such a serious, sombre religion. The only humour in Marx's own writings derives from scathing satire or bitter irony. Maybe if we are really alone in this universe, and have to make for ourselves whatever salvation we can, there is not much to be light-hearted about. At least seriousness is better than the empty bantering of the secularists, who chase after happiness as a distraction from the search for joy. Most humour derives from incongruity: mistaken identity, double meanings, embarrassing situations etc. Animals play, but only human beings have humour — probably because we are incongruous beings in this universe to start with.

Transcendentalists can afford to be light-hearted, because they do not believe that the incongruity of personal being in an impersonal universe is the final word about reality. Perhaps our sense of humour is actually an echo from transcendental reality — another indicator of its being. At least this would make us feel sufficiently secure to take the occasional laugh at ourselves, something Marxists seem to find impossible.

11 Transcendental religion

PANTHEISM AND THEISM

If you want to describe the difference between an aeroplane and a bus, you can do it in bold, broad outlines or fine detail. Both are transport vehicles, but the simplest way to describe the difference is to say that one flies through the air on wings and the other rolls along the ground on wheels. Depending on your purpose, this might be enough. Of course if you were a transport planner, you may want to look at other differences: speed, fuel efficiency, crew requirements etc. A design engineer may be interested in different construction details: engine tolerances, mental stress, power-to-weight ratios and so on.

Now transcendental religions are all different. It is possible to explore these differences in broad outline or fine detail too. This is not a book about comparative religion; rather its purpose is to discover the truest and deepest explanation of reality and human identity.[1] Therefore it will be concerned only with the big, important differences between the transcendental religions. There is nothing devious about this method — we use it in other areas of life all the time.

Take politics for example. We all know that the modern world tends to divide politically between some kind of socialism and some kind of capitalism. Yet, within these two broad types, there are literally thousands of detailed variations. But most people know what the major and significant differences are and most people have made up their minds one way or the other.

Amongst the main transcendental religions there are two basic divisions too. On the one side there is some sort of pantheism (Hinduism and Buddhism).[2] And on the other side there is some sort of theism (Judaism, Islam and Christianity).

The real enemy

Before we explore these differences, it needs to be said that all these religions agree about the fundamental reality and importance of supratranscend-

1. As this book is intended to be popular and non-academic, I have tried to avoid footnotes. But because people find the differing claims of the transcendental religions so confusing, I want to break my rule and refer to another book. For a more detailed discussion of the point of view I am putting forward, see Stephen Neill's **Christian Faith and Other Faiths,** Oxford University Press, 1977.
2. It is true that both Buddhism and Hinduism can take theistic forms, but in each case pantheism appears to be the purer form of religion.

ental being. I have no intention of engaging in any cheap point scoring off the religions with which I happen to disagree. But I cannot accept the muddy-minded secularist point of view that all transcendental religions are basically the same. This popular opinion demonstrates that the people who hold it do not know much about transcendental religions. Secularists offer it as a cheap and easy solution to the problem of relativism. But, as any transcendentalist knows, this view has become one of the greatest excuses ever invented for avoiding personal and moral commitment to the transcendental reality they hold dear. If secularists were really concerned to find the truth about reality and identity, instead of living in a phantasy world, they would know that these religions were not basically the same at all.

Transcendental religions should be expending their vital energies combatting the phantasies of secularism, and their quieter energies in frank and honest discussion with each other. It would be a great tragedy, for example, if Western Christianity exhausted itself in hostile disputes with other transcendentalists, even with Marxism, but failed to see that the secularism within and around it posed the greatest threat. Western secularism is the most meaningless and morally bankrupt religion in the modern world. It seems to me that the first task of Western Christianity is to disentangle itself from the mindless trivia, comsumer greed, selfish pleasure-seeking and 'profits before people' mentality of Western secularism. Christian transcendentalism has already lost its cutting edge of Western countries, because it remains over-identified with the hollow secularism which has thrown off its spiritual mantle.

There are, of course, sincere and well-meaning people who genuinely want to syncretize the various transcendental religions into one great religion. Followers of Bahai are a well-known example. They are not trying to avoid commitment to transcendental reality, but are genuinely trying to find a way through the maze of transcendental religions. The fact that Bahai has attracted relatively few followers does not itself prove anything, but syncretism is based on an erroneous conception.

When six leading astronomers all offer competing theories about the origin and nature of black holes, nothing is gained by a seventh party mixing them all up into one great astronomical stew. Reason would suggest that, of all the theories, this mixture is the most likely to be false. It is more likely that one of the original theories was true, or near to the truth, although some of the others probably had truth in them too. But only further thought and encounter with reality (i.e. research) could sort out truth from error. It is the same with transcendental religions. To think you can make one true religion by stirring a bit of each into a theological pot is like throwing a few pages of every great novel into a lottery barrel in the hope of producing a best-seller.

In the past, religions have come and gone as richer, more accurate interpretations of reality replaced them. Nobody now worships the gods of the ancient Egyptian, Babylonian or Roman empires — to name just a few of the more striking examples. Yet even in those ancient times a tiny, insignificant people we now call Jews worshipped a God who today, through Judaism, Christianity and Islam, is worshipped by a majority of the world's population. No natural explanation seems to account for the survival of Israel's God through the rise and fall of great empires and their deities. Jews, Christians and Muslims would all agree that only his greater reality can explain this God's survival amidst the economic, military and cultural power supporting the religions of the great pagan empires.

What we now call the great world religions have roots going far back into history, some as far back as the dawn of recorded history itself. Each has faced and survived the challenge of other interpretations of reality. But in the modern world they are, in a new and unique way, faced with each other. In the past, these great world religions have sometimes sought to convert each other and sometimes, sadly, fought with each other. But in more recent times they have, like huge bears, mostly kept to their own territory and lived in their own lairs — except when they have been converting animists or followers of other simple religions.

Mass education, modern communication and travel are now bringing these religions face to face in a new way. The world is slowly becoming a global village, producing the relativized consciousness we looked at in an earlier chapter. All things being equal, we can expect relativism to become a global, and not merely Western, problem. We have seen that secularism and syncretism are two shallow and inadequate attempts to solve the relativist dilemma. But what is the solution?

The way ahead

As the solution lies in future history, we cannot be certain what the answer will be. But from past history we can be fairly certain of some things. For example, we can be sure that the future lies with some form of transcendental religion — because, given what we know already, no other explanation of reality can adequately account for the totality of human experience, especially the experience of being a transcendent self. Thus, in the long run, we might expect secularism and Marxism to die out, unless they are kept alive by massive self-deception or naked power.

As many transcendental religions have died out in the past, fading away in the face of a deeper, truer transcendental religion, we might expect some of the now great world religions to die out too. It is reasonable to assume that one or other of the great world religions offers a deeper and truer interpretation of reality than the others. But because it is likely the technological revolution will draw more and more people into the relativized consciousness of the global village, secularist phantasy religion may enjoy a temporary boom. When the discovery of secularism's meaning and moral vacuity bursts that boom, ex-secularists will be able to choose the religion which most adequately copes with human experience — without social background predisposing them towards a particular religion.

All this is speculation, so let us move from distant possibilities and concentrate on the present. Pantheism and theism are the major differences between the transcendental religions. In the end, pantheistic religions see supratranscendental being as impersonal. This is true for Hinduism and Buddhism, although both concede belief in personal deity for their more simple and childish followers. Theistic religions view supratranscendental reality as personal — *a* transcendental Being, not just transcendental being.

This is not an unimportant difference, a mere theological quibble. Most people think it important to understand the nature of electricity, a somewhat less crucial matter than the transcendental. We do not all need to be experts on the subject, but an elementary knowledge of electricity allows us to use its power without endangering ourselves. And an advanced knowledge of electricity allows the experts to benefit us with light, power and communications. It would be foolish to disregard the nature of transcendental reality because, to put it crudely, the more we know about it, the more we can benefit from it.

In an earlier chapter we noted the amazing ability of human beings to work out the nature of the 'out there' universe in their head, and then later to discover that what they worked out was true. The example cited was Einstein, who reasoned that if atoms were split, incredible amounts of energy would be released. The same process works for other scientists too. Astronomers are able to use reason to predict the existence of stars they then find with their telescopes. Now if we are to decide between theism and pantheism, we might first work out what reason leads us to expect, and then look around to see if there is any reality which corresponds to it.

We have discovered that human beings are, in one very important sense, aliens in their world. The alien self is personality — what we have usually called the transcendent self. This alien self is always searching for its real identity, or trying to run away from its own reality into a world of half or total phantasy. But phantasy is no solution. Personality is either a tragic cosmic accident which, as we have seen, does not accord with reason, or it has its real purpose and being in a supratranscendental reality. We have seen that not only does reason suggest the latter, but also that there are definite pointers towards this reality within our own transcendent selves.

Pure reason would therefore lead us to expect that, whatever else this supratranscendental reality is like, it at least must be personal. Otherwise the centre of human being, our spiritual personality, would remain lost and alien. We would be thrown back to a new version of the old cosmic hiccup theory again, except that personality would now be a spiritual rather than a material accident. And if the transcendental reality was less than personal, we would be greater than it — at least in the sense of being more highly developed beings.

Yet we could reasonably expect a supratranscendental Being to be personal on a much higher level than ourselves. I sometimes think the appallingly crude pictures of an 'old man in the sky', used by some theists, make the idea of supratranscendental personality incredible to many people. We will look into this matter in *Part Three*. For the moment it is sufficient to note we must never confuse mere pictures with the actual reality of a supratranscendental Being. It would be reasonable to expect that its personality might exceed our own experience of personality as much as our consciousness exceeds a potato's. In fact Christianity claims just this. Its strange and seemingly contradictory idea of a triune unity — one in three and three in one — suggests that supratranscendental personality is far more complex than ours.

Of course if there is no evidence for the actual reality of a personal supratranscendental Being, then reason's expectations will be proved false. In a moment we shall have to ask what kind of evidence we might expect to find and whether there is any or not. First we must discover why pantheists believe that this Being is impersonal.

The pantheist solution

Like all transcendentalists, pantheists know that only supratranscendental reality can explain the totality of human experience and provide us with a real identity. They know also that we seem to be cut off from this reality, and feel lost and alien. Like theists, pantheists see that the spiritual personality is our problem. Everything else we know, from trees and rabbits to ink-wells and planets, seems to fulfil its being as part of nature. Indeed, if like humans other beings actually 'rose above' nature and knew that they were part of it, they would feel lost and alien too.

So pantheism decides that if spiritual personality is the problem, it must be eliminted — by the same kind of fusion with spiritual reality that other beings have with nature. This certainly seems to solve the problem, but at the cost of denying and negating the very thing that makes us human in the first place. Try as I have, I must confess that I fail to see the difference between this mystical, spiritual absorption and sheer nothingness.

Belief in the impersonal nature of supratranscendental reality has some rather unreasonable and unfortunate consequences for everyday life. These consequences are similar to those of the philosophized Christianity of Hegel, which we looked at in the last chapter. Secularists believe that the everyday world is the only reality, but pantheists do not believe that it is a reality at all, just an illusion. They seek escape from everyday reality in body-denying asceticism and personality-denying meditation. The result is that little concern is taken to improve the human lot in the everyday world. Unless they have already been partly secularized, pantheists remain disinterested in science and technology, even in the truly beneficial sides of it. They tend to accept that what is, is what is meant to be.

With Hinduism, this has resulted in a caste system producing gross economic and social inequality, which Hinduism itself is powerless to change. Pantheists also tend to ignore history, and thus fail to understand the past which has made them what they are. History is just part of the illusory world of everyday life, a world from which one must seek release in other-worldly mysticism.

If the desire for basic economic growth continues to introduce science and technology to the pantheistic countries then, unless there are some basic modifications to belief, it is hard to see how pantheism could survive the enormous changes that would ensue. Pantheistic religions also remain incredibly vulnerable to the Marxist critique of religion; thus it is not surprising to see the growth of Marxism in some pantheistic societies.

Because they have spent so much time and effort trying to eliminate the *I* or ego sense of the self, pantheists have made some nearly unsurpassed discoveries about human psychology. In an earlier chapter we discovered that everyday reality was comprised of at least four types of being — *it*, *me*, *you* and *I*. The meditative techniques of pantheists, especially Zen Buddhists, produce some of the best resolutions to *it* and *me* tensions available.

In every cell of our bodies, each human being is a part of nature. When this *it* part of the self is in communion with the roots of its own being (nature), we experience a marvellous sense of serenity. We all seek this kind of peace. Some of us find it by the sea, at the countryside, in the mountains or our own gardens. I experience it most in a limestone cave, with its ancient flow-stones, stalagmites and stalactites. I feel that part of me belongs there — needs to be there — in the depths of the earth. With meditation techniques one can achieve this sense of *it* to *it* communion in the heart of a huge city, where even asphalt and concrete become its vehicles.

Other tensions derive from conflict within us, between mind and body, consciousness and unconsciousness (*me* to *it* and *me* to *me* tensions). Pantheist meditation techniques work superbly here too, perhaps better than secularist techniques involving drug therapy and psycho-analysis. For example, yogis can reduce their blood pressure, a hyper-tension problem all too familiar to frenetic, secularized Westerners, by using meditation techniques. The use of mantras — words you repeat over and over again, until you lose all sense of anything but the mantra itself — can bring an enormous sense of inner harmony, relieving *me* to *me* tensions.

But you do not have to be a pantheist, or even a transcendentalist, to learn and use these techniques. Nor do you have to pay large sums of money to some half-Westernized guru to teach you. Most libraries are now well stocked with books which teach the art of meditation minus its pantheistic overtones. Secularists and theists, even Marxists, can easily incorporate meditation into their way of life without becoming pantheistic transcendentalists.

The theist solution and the example of personal relationships

But pantheists and theists part ways completely when they come to the *I* and *you* types of being. For pantheists the *I* or ego, with all its desires, must be extinguished. Like a drop of water, it must be absorbed mystically into the great sea of transcendental being. The reunion of the individual transcendent self with its supratranscendental source is to be achieved by each pantheist willing away every trace of his/her separate existence.

For theists the problem is not the ego itself, but wilfully immoral ego. And the initiative towards reunion between the human spirit and the supratranscendental Spirit is not made by us, but by it itself. Whilst not denying its mystical qualities, theists speak of relationship with, rather than absorption into, the supratranscendental Being. We can see the greater reasonableness of the theistic expectation when we reflect upon communion between the transcendent selves we already know well, the relationships we share with other human beings.

If two people have recently 'fallen in love', they tend to idealize the depth of communion they share with each other (the *I* to *you* communion). Each feels so completely understood by the other, that they feel their sentences could be finished off for them or their thoughts read. A few years of marriage or living together soon destroys their illusion. We call these familiar experiences 'romantic'; they seem to arise from intense sexual attraction and a deep need to be understood by someone. But the understanding is a phantasy projection and, when we finally see the other person as they really are, we often blame them cruelly for not being what we had phantasized them to be.

If divorce or separation is not to follow, and the same process repeated all over again with someone else, two hard lessons will need to be learnt. First, there must be continuous self-revelation of the inner thoughts and feelings of each to the other. Personal being, the *I*, is a peculiarly revelatory being. Without cues of conversation, of sign and body language, even of sighs and groans, human beings cannot commune with each other. Indeed we have the capacity for great personal concealment or deception. This is why the social (human) sciences will never reach the precision of the natural sciences — they are dealing with subjects, not just objects.

The second lesson to be learnt is morality. No satisfactory relationship can exist between human beings unless the other is loved as much as one's own self. In practice this will mean that certain things must be done and certain things must not be done, but it must also include the capacity to forgive when the agreements are broken. Without self-revelation and positive moral behaviour there can be no communion between human beings.

If supratranscendental reality is personal, as theists believe, then reason should lead us to expect it to reveal itself. Otherwise we could never know it, especially if it does not normally reside in some kind of body open to our sensory perceptions. But even if it does reveal itself, to know it we would have to 'tune in' to its self-revelation (an *I* to *I* communion). Failure to 'tune in' would have a similar result to those human relationships where people do not listen to each other.

Yet this revelation would have to be more substantial than the rather vague traces of its being we have already discovered on the journey into human identity. Those hints leave us more lost than found. But perhaps it has some purpose in remaining somewhat vague to us. It could also be that the vagueness of its being derives from something within ourselves — from something *we* have done. Maybe we have distanced ourselves from it by behaving wrongly towards it, just as we destroy communion with human friends or relatives by acting immorally against them.

Now this is exactly what theists claim has happened. They say that God has revealed himself, but with a certain amount of purposeful veiledness, and that all human beings have behaved immorally towards him. If God seems far away, the theists say, it is we who have made the move. In *Part Three* we shall look more deeply into these matters.

From now on I shall use the English name *God* for the personal supratranscendental Being — a rather easier term to handle! But I think you will see the point of all the previous jargon. I shall also use the pronoun *he*, but this does not imply that God is male. Unfortunately English does not have a combined-gender personal pronoun. The question of God's sex will also have to wait until *Part Three*.

The great theistic religions — Judaism, Islam and Christianity — all agree that God has revealed himself. They also agree that the religious experience of the Jewish people, passed on in oral tradition from the dawn of recorded history and coming down to modern times in written form as the Jewish Bible (the Christian Old Testament), was such a revelation. But they disagree about the process of revelation beyond this point.

Christians believe that Jesus, himself a Jew, was the long-awaited Jewish Messiah (or Christ), the human incarnation of God. Modern Judaism is comprised of the descendents of those Jews who did not accept that Jesus was the Messiah. Today they usually accept Jesus as one of their great spiritual teachers, but in one way or other they still wait for God to reveal his Messiah. Muslims accept Jesus as a prophet of the divine Being, but not as great a prophet as Muhammad.

In essence, the three religions worship the same God. But their differences are not mere speculative quibbles; they are basic differences over the nature of God and about how to get in touch with him. The best way to make up your own mind about these differences is to read and compare for yourself the Old Testament, the Koran and the New Testament.

The history of relationships between the disciples of these religions is a sorry tale of that elemental evil which each believes has distorted and manacled human personality. Modern disciples must view this history with a deep sense of sin and repentance, especially on the part of Muslims and Christians. The differences between the three religions are very real, but this must not become an excuse for avoiding personal commitment to the God they seek to follow. For their own part, each religion needs to see that the pointless use of violence and persecution to 'persuade' the others only fosters secularist phantasies and Marxist antitranscendentalism. A thousand good arguments are destroyed by one failure to practise what one preaches.

* * *

We have now come to the end of the second part of this journey. It has not been a journey uncovering the minute detail one might see by riding on a bike or in a motor car. Rather it has been a journey showing only the detail one might see from a light plane or helicopter. Simplification has been a necessary ally; where simplification has turned into distorted over-simplification I can only apologize to those I have offended. But it is the intention of this book to give large signposts to people who have to travel, but hardly know where to begin — people who do not know where they are now.

At the end of *Part One* we discovered that the problem of identity is a religious problem. We saw that modern people have a choice between three kinds of religion: worldly, inner-worldly and transcendental. It became clear that everyone is religious, but the problem is which religion is true or truest?

In *Part Two* we discovered that relativism has deepened, but certainly not abolished this difficult question. We saw that of the three choices only worldly-religion contains virtually no truth at all. It is just an escapist phantasy which tries to side-step the problem of identity through self-deception. The only identity secularism has to offer is the shallow 'natural attitude' identity Eva Adamson gave to the questioner at the party (chapter 1).

Then we saw that some form of transcendentalism appears to offer the fullest explanation of our total experience of reality. We noted Marxism (inner-worldly religion) has some important truths to say to demonically distorted forms of transcendental religion which ignore bodies, bellies and history. But in itself Marxism is dangerous, ignoring the depths of personal evil and abolishing the only ground by which Marxism itself might be judged.

Finally we saw that some form of theism seems to be the truest kind of transcendentalism — that the root source of reality must itself be personal. If this is so, then in order to be known the personal transcendent Being must reveal itself to us. Persons are not objects we study with our eyes, either by looking down microscopes, up telescopes or any other way.

Part Three will assume that the divine revelation unveiled by Jesus Christ is the deepest, truest disclosure of ultimate reality and identity presently available to human beings. I have thought it best to let the reasons behind this assumption unfold as we journey into Christianity itself. Where it is relevant or important to do so, I shall try to show why Christianity enshrines a deeper and truer revelation of God than Judaism or Islam.

I hope that the claim for the unique position of Christianity among the religions will be read with the humility that is intended towards the truths the others preserve. I am not interested in scoring points, winning arguments or, I hope, being fearfully defensive in the psychological sense. But I cannot accept the weak-mindedness and selfish rationalizations that lie behind pure relativism or the empty phantasies of secularism. For the other religions I have nothing but respectful disagreement, and the interest to present the truth as I see it after my own journeying into the mystery of being human.

Part Three:

The Christian way

12

Maps of reality

THE VALIDITY OF SPIRITUAL EXPERIENCE

'It's just a lot of words, a lot of fancy talk about nothing.'

This is how a scientist described theology to me recently. I sympathized with his sentiment. For a lot of people theology is just words, because it has not been related to their experience. The ancients believed that words had power. And words do have power too, but not the superstitious power the ancients believed in — the power of magic incantations, or the power to make a child rich or happy by merely giving it a name meaning 'rich' or 'happy'. The power of words is the power to 'rise above' the fog of experience — to name it, understand it, direct it, find your way through it.

The ancients were not fools, but our probing of reality often surpasses theirs. They observed that when a stone was thrown into the air, it fell back to earth with ever increasing acceleration. But why? They said it was because the spirit in the stone became more and more joyful the closer it approached the centre of the universe — its home, the earth. Today we smile at such tales — not at the ancients' experience which is the same as ours, but at the word maps they used to explain it. We find no evidence to suggest that a stone has a spirit inside it. And we know that the earth is not even at the centre of our own galaxy, let alone of the universe. For us, modern physics provides better maps with words like 'density', 'mass' or 'gravitational field'.

What we call science is really a map or series of maps of the 'out there' reality. We trust modern science because its maps seem to accurately chart our real experiences of that reality. If you go into a chemistry laboratory, you will probably see atomic-weight charts hanging on the wall. These charts are word and number maps of the structure of the various chemical substances. You may even see three-dimensional models based upon these maps — little coloured balls joined with connecting rods, arranged to represent the molecular structure of each chemical.

For the past two hundred years scientists have used these maps to find their way through chemical reality. Unashamedly working with a map of a reality they had never actually seen, chemical scientists performed experiments, produced disease-combatting drugs and synthesized new metals and plastics for technological application. From their experience of the things they could see, scientists knew the molecular maps fairly precisely represented the reality they could not see. Only the development of the electron microscope in the last couple of decades has made direct confirmation of the molecular maps possible.

Theology: a guide to experience

Theology is a map of spiritual experience. But we must never confuse maps with the reality they represent. When I go bush-walking, for safety reasons I like to have a map of the reality I intend to trek through. Now it is one thing to sit with that map spread across my desk at home, planning a journey crossing dark, black lines symbolizing rivers or a row of spidery asterisks representing a mountain range. It is quite another thing to wade across those rivers and get your pack wet or, with panting breath, struggle for a foothold near the peak of those ranges. The map is an abstraction from a rich reality, a useful representation based on someone else's experience. But the map has neither the dangers nor the delight of the actual reality itself. No mere map can provide the panoramic splendour of the view from a mountain top, or the satisfaction of conquering tired muscles and treacherous slopes to get there.

Theology is a map of the most exciting and dangerous journey of all, the journey of the personal, spiritual life of human beings through this present world of space and time. Its map is grounded in the reality we have come to call the transcendent self or 'spiritual personality'. Like many people today, my scientist friend had been blinded to his experience of personal spiritual reality; he thought theology was a map of nothing. To him theology was what words praising a sunset must be to a man born blind.

If we want it, the windows of spiritual perception can be wiped clean. But not wanting this insight does not mean we do not need it. By far the greatest threat to human life and values in this world today is ourselves. By comparison with his forbears, modern man is a giant of material power. But his demonic obsession with the 'out there' reality is slowly turning him into a spiritual dwarf. What our spiritual blindness may mean in another life will have to wait for later. But Jesus Christ taught that spiritual blindness was inexcusable — 'Having eyes, you do not see', he said.

Theology is a map rooted in the cumulative spiritual experience of generation after generation of men and women making their personal pilgrimage from birth to death. It is grounded first in a reality everybody undeniably experiences, the reality of personal transcendence. But that is only the beginning. It is also grounded in experiential encounters with the being of God himself. Some of these encounters are especially valued because they have happened to men and women of spiritual genius — to patriarchs, prophets and apostles. But they have been confirmed in the experience of countless millions of ordinary men and women too. Because these encounters experience God as a person, they are always described as *revelations*.

Now the idea of revelation is not foreign to science either. Scientific genius never discovers anything that was not already there in the 'out there' universe; it simply unveils it. But a scientific discovery is only considered to be true if it can be confirmed by experience, by anyone being able to reproduce the results of the claimed experiment or observation.

Divine revelation involves two steps: our movement towards God and God's movement towards us. But theology claims that the reality it maps is open to everyone's experience too. Jesus Christ said, 'He who seeks shall find'. If this is true — and only willingness to experience, not just to theorize, can tell — then, if we do not seek God, we will not find him. Later we shall see why this is so. But we should note that the word Jesus used was *seek*, not 'take an odd glance' or 'grope around a bit'. Spiritual genius is a quality possessed by those who have sought much and been much found.

Christian theology has three main maps: Roman Catholic, Eastern Orthodox and Protestant. But these maps share a basic common core. Before the rise of secularism and Marxism, Christians could afford the luxury of disputing over their differences. But now they are coming to realize that necessities must come before luxuries. In this book I will be concerned only with necessities, with the core map of Christian experience. Sometimes this is called orthodox or catholic (small 'c') Christianity; it is summarized in the Apostles' Creed.

From time to time all sorts of people pop up claiming to have experienced a new and truer revelation of God than the one mapped by orthodoxy. Usually they are university professors or cranks, and invariably what they call 'new' is some dead end which orthodoxy discarded centuries ago. This may seem a surprising or unkind statement; after all new discoveries in science are being made all the time. But science deals with objects, and its discoveries depend entirely on human ability and effort. Theology depends on God's self-revelation and, according to theology, the revelation made by Jesus Christ is the yardstick by which to measure all other revelations. That is why a knowledge of the history of Christian theology shows that spiritual genius builds on what orthodoxy knows already, calls Christians back to their Founder's teaching or translates orthodoxy afresh for a new generation.

Christianity and modern knowledge

There are some Christians who reject orthodoxy and claim that theology must accommodate itself to modern knowledge. But of all knowledge, that which is usually called *modern* knows least about personal and moral being. To suggest that Christianity should accommodate itself to this is like asking a fish to make itself at home in the desert.

So-called modern knowledge is usually a muddle-headed mishmash of half-digested science and secularism. As we have seen, theology can accept the real discoveries of modern science without needing to accommodate itself to anything. Theology's attitude to secularism should be caring confrontation, not unwitting accommodation. Secularized Christians have been dazzled by a false analogy with modern technology, believing that *new* means 'best'. Secularism is certainly newer than Christianity, but chronological snobbery provides no test for the depth of reality in religion.

Some people are wary of theology because they think that, being based on revelation, it must be unreasonable or irrational. They think that theology asks them to throw away their minds and take a blind leap of faith, like jumping over a cliff and hoping to fly. But this view is based on a serious misunderstanding. I suspect it arises because of all the crank theologies which are obviously the product of manipulative exploiters or sad, little dreamers.

Christian theology is certainly based on revelation, but it does not debunk reason. On the contrary, theology claims to show the real basis of reason in the mind of God, and to expose the folly of magic and superstition. We have seen that science not only discovers rational order in the 'out there' reality, but also that scientific reasoning — the human mind — can actually predict things about that reality which it has not yet seen or experienced. We also saw that science cannot explain reason, but it knows that it works.

Now Christian theology says that human reason works because it was made by a God of infinite reason. It says also that scientists can understand and predict the nature of the 'out there' universe because it did not derive from chance, but was made and structured by God's reason. But even in this world, the higher we go up the structure of being, the more we have to depend on the object being studied actually revealing itself. Rocks sit still while the geologist pokes at them, but forest birds fly away from the ornithologist. Human beings can pour out their thoughts and feelings to social scientists or remain silent.

To understand personal being, including human behaviour, the subject must reveal an inner self which is impenetrable to scientific reason and observation. Theology believes that reason can take us to the point where we know that God exists, but only revelation can tell us what he is like and how we can make contact with him.

The first two parts of this book have taken us to the limits of reason's ability to penetrate into the mystery of being human. They have applied to our modern situation what Paul the Apostle said to the tiny Christian church in Rome about AD 58. He claimed that every human being really knows, deep down, that God is real. Why?

First, says St Paul, because nothing in the 'out there' universe explains its intricate design or the origin of human transcendence. St Paul put it this way:

> *What can be known about God is plain to them, because God has shown it to them. Ever since the creation of the world his invisible nature, namely his eternal power and deity, has been clearly perceived in the things that have been made* (Romans 1:19-20).

Second, we know God's reality because of moral conscience. We know that however much the details of morality might vary from age to age and society to society, there is a real difference between good and evil. And we know that we are held accountable for our own moral behaviour. For St Paul human beings exist in a reality where:

> *their conscience also bears witness, and their conflicting thoughts accuse or perhaps excuse them on that day when . . . God judges the secrets of men* (Romans 2:15-16).

The third part of this book will take us on a journey into spiritual reality as mapped by the

Christian revelation of God. Far from being unreasonable or illogical, this revelation will uncover the mysteries that reason already dimly knows.

13

From nothing to something

CHRISTIANITY AND CREATION

Who made God? What is God like? Why did God make us? Where is God? These are some of the deep and important questions theology answers. But we must see how these answers relate to human experience, otherwise they will seem remote and unreal.

Today scientists tend to favour the 'big bang' theory about the origins of the universe. They think everything began with a great cosmic explosion and has gone on expanding ever since. Perhaps tomorrow they will favour some other theory. But Christianity is not concerned with the *how* and *when* of creation; it is content to leave such matters to scientific theorizing. Christianity is concerned with the *who* and *why* of creation — with personal life, with the human spirit. According to Christian revelation, God originally created the whole universe from nothing.

If the scientific theories are right, it appears by

human standards that God spent a long time creating the conditions in which he wanted self-conscious human spirit to emerge. But if time means anything to God, which it may not, to him the whole process we call evolution probably seemed to take about a millisecond. Fifty years ago a statement like this would have caused people to giggle in unbelief, but now even our own electronic creations transmit pictures and perform complex mathematical calculations in milliseconds.

From our end of the process, creation looks like the gradual unfolding of a great musical symphony. The first movement is the intricate and subtle arrangement of matter, which slowly produces that piece of sheer artistry we call the human body — with all its sensitive sensors trailing to the brain. For a long time human-like creatures seem to roam the earth possessed of consciousness, but not self-consciousness.

Then at some time in the not-so-distant past the second movement breaks forth, entwining two new rapturous themes with the primal rhythms of the first movement. One theme is the emergence of self-conscious spirit in human bodies, worked perhaps through some delicate shift in the material construction of the brain. We may never know how the divine artist moulds the creation of personal spirit in matter, because all the brains of the non-self-conscious humanoids have rotted away, making comparison impossible. What we do know is that self-conscious spirit quavers inside our own bodies as the very centre of the self.

The second movement's other theme is the sound

of the divine artist himself. Alongside the emergence of self-conscious human spirits comes also consciousness of God. No 'primitive' tribe known to humankind lacks some kind of awareness of God.

How did we begin?

But let us descend from creation's cosmic symphony to our own lives here in the earth, where this whole process is repeated inside ourselves. Life began for each one of us in unconsciousness. We retain no self-conscious memory of the period of foetal growth spent inside our mothers' wombs. The Bible picturesquely describes this as the time:

> *when I was being made in secret, intricately wrought in the depths of the earth* (Psalm 138:15).

Conceived in pleasure and born in pain, we were already surrounded by the mysterious paradoxes of life as, involuntarily, we left the womb for the world. Soom we became conscious, feebly groping for mother's breast, smiling at familiar loving faces, startled by sharp sounds and strange surroundings. Without special training, our parents coaxed and coached us into their language and customs. In this subtle clod of matter we call the body, self-consciousness began to emerge. We learnt that in one profound and disturbing sense we had become a tiny circle of self-conscious aloneness in a vast whirling world of matter and time. The birth of spirit in matter, which seems to have taken aeons to occur in the universe, was reproduced in us within the space of a few short years. God made us too, as Christianity says, out of nothing.

Some years before I accepted Christianity, I

remember being at the movies when the film projector broke down. There must have been something wrong with its motor, because it stopped suddenly, leaving one frame clearly projected on to the screen. While the projectionist worked to get the machine going again, the intense light focussed on this single, still frame burnt it out. In fact through a succession of fitful starts and stops, the same thing happened six or seven times. On each occasion the coloured scene appearing on the screen smokelessly dissolved in an irregular pattern from the centre outwards, until it was a blank, white nothing.

I remember the experience clearly because each time it happened I was overcome by a feeling of nauseous dread. It seemed to start in the pit of my stomach. Then it would work its way through my whole body, finally surfacing as a cold, clammy sweat. At the time I could not make any sense of it. I had never had such an experience before. I remember wondering if I was coming down with some kind of serious illness. Later, when I realized there was nothing physically the matter with me, I recall thinking that although the experience was horrible it was also, somehow, important. But I did not know why.

Years passed before I realized that on that night at the movies I had experienced the horror of not being, of nothingness. The dissolution of the richly-coloured world projected on to the screen had reflexively mirrored a truth about my own inner life. I had experienced some kind of half-reflection of the nothingness from which I came, the nothingness which, without God, I would fall back into again.

Many times since, usually during late night conversations, friends have told of similar experiences occurring in entirely different circumstances. Together we have come to the conclusion that nightmares about falling with nothing to land on are expressing the same truth about human being. Perhaps some people so effectively guard themselves against this knowledge that it only comes to them in the passive state of dream consciousness.

God, history and humans

We do not know when the human animal first became a self-conscious spirit. But, until this happened, there was no more likelihood of a human history developing than a horse history or a mouse history. Only transcendent beings have history.

Right from the beginning of recorded human history, the people we today call Jews were grasped by the idea that matter and time originated in spirit. At least from the days of Abraham, at the start of the second millenium before Christ, the Jews were seized by a vision of the history of matter and the human spirit as part of a great divine plan. The sense of this plan grew and unfolded down the centuries through patriarchs and prophets to Christ and the apostles, and now lives in the activities that take place in our local church every Sunday.

But even before recorded history, the beautiful biblical story of Adam and Eve had been passed down by word of mouth for generations. Eventually it was written down to become the prelude to the Old Testament. This story is not history, science or fairy-tale, but dramatized theology. It reveals with clarity what all of us already dimly know — that God brought us into being from nothing. But it also discloses what no human being could ever know without revelation — that God made the whole universe from nothing too.

It seems strange to say that God made everything out of nothing. Creation itself is no stranger to human experience, but creation from nothing is. Creativity is a sign of the presence of self-conscious spirit. Animals seem to create almost entirely from instinct, repeating the same patterns generation after generation. But human beings are enormously inventive. Artists create new pictures, engineers new machines, writers new novels and poems, chemists new synthetics and so on. But human creation always uses *pre-existent* materials, shaping and fashioning them into new combinations. When Christianity says that God made the world from nothing, it means that he first invented the materials themselves and then shaped and fashioned them.

No theologian would claim that the idea of creation from nothing is easy to understand. If someone wanted to invent a popular religion, they would probably find the idea that God used some kind of already existing material more widely appealing. That is the kind of creation we are used to. But if this was true, and thus Christian revelation wrong, we would have to conclude that some kind of substance lay outside God's power and control. It would be like saying there were two Gods — one a great, creative self-conscious Spirit and the other an immense but inert, 'down-pulling' blob. With this dualism we could never be sure which side would get control, or whether they would battle endlessly without result.

Our own experience of the recalcitrance of matter — from the fight to prevent our own houses from crumbling to dust, to the scientific calculations that the sun will eventually burn itself out — makes dualism seem quite plausible. But if matter was not invented by God, there is no guarantee that it won't overcome him, and even less guarantee that it won't overcome material-spiritual beings like us.

At the centre of Christianity is the belief that God incarnated himself in the human person of Jesus Christ. Later we will have to look at the reasons for this belief. But central to all the records about Jesus, and apparently not even doubted by his enemies, is the claim that he could perform nature miracles — giving sight to the blind, stilling a fierce storm, multiplying loaves of bread and rising from the dead. Secularized Christians try to play down the miraculous element in Jesus' life because it upsets the secular mentality which they want to convince of the truth of Christianity. But, all preconceptions apart, there is absolutely no philosophical or scientific reason why miracles cannot occur.

In fact, as St Paul said long ago, Christianity stands or falls on one miracle — the resurrection of Jesus Christ from the dead. If that did not happen, then Christians should be pitied for living by a hope based in delusion. Without the nature miracles, especially the resurrection, the Christian belief about creation would lack substance.

Not that these miracles by themselves prove the truth of Christianity; people will always find ways to dismiss anything that contradicts their own preconceived ideas about reality. For this reason Christ always refused to perform miraculous tricks for those who merely wanted proof (see Matthew 12:39). He knew they could explain them away somehow. But if on other grounds we already have reason to believe that a personal, self-conscious Spirit is the source and centre of all reality, then nature miracles are exactly what we might expect to accompany a self-disclosure of that Spirit.

Who made God?

But who made God himself? Where did God come from anyway? These are questions Christianity is always being asked. In one sense the answer is very simple. Christianity says that no one made God and he did not come from anywhere. Or, to put the answer positively, God always was, God is now and God always will be. In other words God cannot be reduced to or explained by anything except himself.

Now this makes good sense. If there was some kind of reality more basic than God, it would be God. The idea of getting down to something you cannot go beyond seems odd at first, but it is not entirely strange to ordinary experience. We all know what colour is — red, blue or yellow — but it is impossible to describe your perception of yellow to a person blind from birth. Colour seems to be just itself. We all know what it is, but we cannot put it into words.

When Christians say that from eternity to eternity God always is, they are simply accepting one of the three possible explanations of reality's roots. Materialists say that some kind of matter is eternal

— that gas or particles have always been there and that the human spirit is just an accidental by-product of matter. The third and never very popular alternative is that reality is one eternal chain of cause and effect, without beginning and without end. Christianity believes in the first alternative because it seems to make the most sense of all human experience, and because it has been confirmed by revelation.

Where is God?

The question Christianity usually gets asked next is: Where is God? But the answer will have to include some information about what God is like too.

When the ancient Byzantine artists of Eastern Orthodox Christianity expressed their faith with brush and oils, they always painted the sky blue and heaven gold. Failure to make this antiquarian distinction has led in modern times to the absurd idea that God exists somewhere up beyond the clouds — that is what Christians are supposed to believe anyway. But the most elementary knowledge of the Christian reality map would dispel this crudity immediately.

Theology has always insisted that God is not an object in the 'out there' reality. Quite the contrary, theology says that the 'out there' reality is an object invented and made by God. The nonsensical view which thinks God is 'up above the sky' has arisen for several reasons. First because in some languages the word 'heaven' can stand either for the sky or for God's own reality dimension — the two are often confused.

Second because the Bible, sensibly, uses poetic

symbols from the sky to try to express an otherwise ineffable sense of where God actually is. I say 'sensibly' because, of all the 'out there' reality, only the sky is big and glorious enough to supply symbols fit to picture the reality dimension of the Creator of all things.

Third, people who do not want to believe in God have found it very convenient to caricature Christianity's map by making out that Christians take the sky symbols of heaven literally.

How then are we to understand where God is? Well, we can begin by thinking again about what God is like. In earlier chapters we saw that Christianity has always believed that God is a person. Now the only persons we know are ourselves. This is why the Bible says that we are the only part of the known universe that really reflects something of what God is like in himself. The creation story in the first book of the Bible says this:

> *So God created man in his own image, in the image of God he created him; male and female he created them* (Genesis 1:27).

Now as long as we spend all our energy exploring the 'out there' reality and ignore persons — the modern folly we discovered in *Part One* — the idea that God is a person will look silly or shallow. It will look like Freud's theory that God is just a phantasy-wish for a super parent. But now that we have journeyed into some of the depths of personal life, this idea begins to take on a new dimension. If we link what we have discovered about persons with the biblical image of humans being made in God's image, we shall find the best way to think of God is *in* and *through* here, not *up* or *out* there.

'In and through here' is another way of saying that the way we experience God is person to person. That is to say the place to find God is in and through your self, not your body — through your transcendent person.

We are, as persons, in our bodies — every part of them. Sometimes we forget that we are in some of the seemingly less important parts, like toes or teeth. But we only have to stub our toe on a step or let a tooth decay to know that we are in toes and teeth, as well as belly and brain.

Christianity says that God is in every particle of the universe too — not in the sense that he is dependent on it for his existence, as we are on our bodies, but in the sense that he makes and keeps the material universe in existence. This is where the pantheists stop. They tell us to go 'in' to the spiritual reality that lies behind the self and the rest of reality, but they stop there. They have no idea of 'through'. As far as pantheism goes, Christianity can agree with it. For example the Old Testament prophet Jeremiah wrote:

> *Do I not fill heaven and earth? says the Lord* (Jeremiah 23:24).

But pantheism does not go far enough; we need 'through' as well as 'in'. Human beings not only experience toothache; they *know* that they experience it too — hence we are able to invent dentistry. Our personality cannot be reduced to our bodies, whether flesh, blood, brains or teeth. As we saw in *Part One*, we are persons because we 'get above' these things.

Now Christianity says that God is 'above' the whole space-time universe, not in the false sense of being 'up' or 'out' there in it, but in the same sense that we 'get above' it. But of course there is this vital difference: God transcends space, time and matter entirely; we only transcend these things a little. But then we are not God; we are only material-spiritual creatures made in his image.

God's total transcendence of the space-time universe is what Christians mean when they say that God is in heaven. This is what the Byzantine painters were also trying to express by painting the sky blue and heaven gold. God is not only in and behind the self and the universe; he is also above and beyond it. The prophet Isaiah put it this way:

> *For as the skies are higher than the earth, so are my ways higher than your ways and my thoughts than your thoughts says the Lord* (Isaiah 55:9).

Because God has made us in a world separate from himself, and as persons separate from his person, we relate to him as one who is through and beyond our self too.

Finding God

Now the idea of relating to God in and through our persons may still be unclear. Let us think of it more directly in terms of the discoveries we made on our journey into human being.

In *Part One* we discovered that becoming a person meant learning that other human beings are not just physical shapes in the 'out there' world (its), but self-conscious persons like ourselves. They not only have bodies separate from us, but also a personal self separate from us. By comparing the monkey boy with Eva Adamson, we discovered that without inter-personal relationships we would remain trapped in nature — conscious, but not self-conscious.

Now rocks have bodily unconsciousness, horses have consciousness in a body, we have self-consciousness without a body — that is why he is invisible to us. A rock has unconsciousness in God and a horse has consciousness in God, but if they know about it at all I presume that it is only as a warm, dull glow — duller for the rock than the horse. Because we participate in 'rock' and 'horse' reality, we have our unconscious bodily life and our conscious mental life in God too. In practical terms this means something like having a healthy kidney and therefore being unaware that we have a kidney at all (rock consciousness), or luxuriating in the breeze blowing across our faces on a hot day without thinking that we are luxuriating in it (horse consciousness). This is where the pantheists want us to stop — with rock and horse-like consciousness in God. It is as far as 'in' without 'through' can go.

In *Part Two* we discovered that human persons can only commune with each other by reaching across the gulf of separateness through mutual self-revelation and mutual love, respect and forgiveness. Even so we never seem able to get as close to people we love as we would like. I suppose that is why parents often express overwhelming feelings of affection for their children by saying 'I'd like to gobble you all up', and why lovers often nibble at each other.

I am not talking about wicked parents and lovers who want to dominate and engulf the subject of their devotion — that form of hate and self-hate that calls dominance or submission 'love'. I mean the desire of genuine love to get closer to the one who is loved but still maintain personal individuality. Later we will have to explore this desire more deeply. For now the key point is one we all already know — that the best personal relationships are a subtle blend of communion and separateness. Separateness without communion is loneliness. Communion without separateness is domination or submission, the one as destructive as the other.

Now finding God through your personal self means relating to him as he is in heaven (his transcendent being), not just relating to him as the One who is in and behind the ordinary space-time world (his immanent being). It is the difference between cuddling someone with whom you also share a deep intimacy of thought and feeling, and cuddling someone you have just met for the first time. The one is a totally personal relationship; the other just a warm physical glow. Like our human personal relationships, we can only have a person-to-person relationship with God when it is based on the revelation of inner-self and on a morality grounded in love, respect and forgiveness.

It is obvious that there will be differences between the relationship of a personal creature with its Creator and the relationships between those creatures themselves, but we will have to leave these differences to later chapters. All that needs to be said here is that we not only find God in but also through the personal self. Thus Christians pray 'Our Father, who art in heaven', not just 'in and behind earth'. The reality hole we called the transcendent self in *Part One* is not a space-time hiccup, but a door into another reality dimension — a door into the only ultimately real reality dimension, God's heaven. What sight, touch, taste, smell and hearing are to the space-time reality, the transcendent self is to heavenly reality. God is not *up* or *out* there in the space time universe; he is *in* and *through* here — in and through the transcendent person he has made us to be.

Why God made us

But why did God make us anyway? This is the question our whole journey has been leading up to.

You can never get the right answers about anything until you ask the right questions. For years scientists searched for a substance called phlogiston, the supposed cause of fire and flame. 'Where is phlogiston?' they asked.

But because they were asking the wrong question (there is no such substance as phlogiston), it took much longer to find the right answer — that fire is caused by the release of combustible gases when an object is heated to the critical temperature.

Now this book began with questions. We called them 'ultimate' questions: Who am I? What is this being alive? What shall I live for and by? What will happen to me when I die? But these are not really the right questions — half right, but not right.

'*Why* did God make us?' is the right question. But, as much as I would have like to, I could not begin with this question — not because I was incapable of typing it down on the page, but because modern people are wary of asking such a religious question. They have learnt not to trust religion, mostly because religion seems not to be based in reality but authority and tradition. They are also wary of religious questions becaue modern science's successful exploration of the 'out there' reality has dazzled them into thinking that answers to personal questions will come from that reality. But now that we have discovered the deep realities religion is based in, we can at last ask the right question: Why did God make us?

Christianity says that God made us for personal communion with himself. Even so-called atheists know that personal relationships between human beings are the most fulfilling experiences ordinary life offers. But Christianity says that this fulfilment is but a reflection of the relationship we were really made for — the relationship with God himself.

To make this relationship possible, God created us as persons separate from himself with a free will of our own. We can use this freedom either to return love to God or to reject him — to say 'No' to the doorway to heaven, even to deny its existence. But this answer is too abstract and theoretical; we must see how it relates to ordinary experience.

It seems that in life's journey each one of us repeats the history of the race as we grow into maturity. We begin with unconsciousness, then comes consciousness and the dimmer beginnings of self-consciousness. Finally, around the time of puberty, we begin to have the capacity to look back on our lives to see the influences that have made us. Until this time it is extraordinarily difficult to tell the difference between reality itself and beliefs which are merely made up by the adults around us.

I remember the shock my daughter felt at seven years of age when she discovered that her friend had come to school without first making her bed.

'Daddy,' said my daughter breathlessly arriving home from school, 'you can't go to school unless you make your bed, can you?' To this sweet innocence I tried to explain that making your bed before going to school was a rule in our house, but that it was not a condition of the universe itself. Generally children find it almost impossible to tell the difference between a rule invented by people they trust and an inalterable condition of reality — like two plus two equals four.

My son has just reached the age of puberty and is beginning to ask questions about his parents' beliefs on many subjects — trying to discover which are real and which are just Mum and Dad's little phantasies. He is, for example, beginning to wonder whether the God to whom we give thanks before meals is real like Mum and Dad say, or unreal like some of his friends' parents and the psychology professor on television say. He is starting to move out of the world under his parents' wings, to a world where he has to make his own decisions. He is becoming a full person quite separate from his mother and father.

Now Christianity says that God made us like this

too. God made us free to accept or reject him, free to live by his rules or our own. He did it because he wanted creatures who could commune with him across the separateness he gave them — a person-to-person relationship of love.

My wife and I are both excited and afraid of our son's growing up. We are excited at the prospect of receiving love from him as a separate adult person and of giving him love in the same way, but afraid that we might stifle his personal growth by being over-protective, keeping him under our wings in immaturity. We are also afraid that he will reject us, that he will not love us.

God, unlike human parents, could have made his human children as robots, programming them to love him without free choice. But he did not, because programmed love would not be love at all. Freedom is love's condition. When my teenage son demonstrates his affection for me, I cherish it as freely-given love. I also like my cat rubbing his body against my legs, but his is not the love of free choice — he 'loves' me because he wants his dinner.

Some parents desperately try never to give their children adult freedom; they want dependent cat-like 'love' even when their offspring have reached adult age. But at best what they get is grudging submission, and at the worst total rebellion or their child's mental breakdown. God has made us sufficiently free of himself either to love or to rebel against him. He did it so that there could be real love between us and him, not just robot 'love' or cowering submission. We were made to find our true fulfilment in a person-to-person relationship of love with God.

Now all this seems perfectly reasonable — it seems to fit the facts of experience discovered on our journey into human being. Except one. *Does* God really love us? If he does, then why has he made us in a world with so much pain and suffering? Christianity faces no harder question than this one. It will be the subject of the next chapter.

* * *

The next chapter will begin to take us on a journey into the Christian revelation of the inner nature of God's person. This chapter has only explored the surface of God's person, but it is the appropriate place to say something about God's sex. We experience human person as two sexes: male and female.

When the Book of Genesis says that God made man in his own image, it defines man as male and female. In other words it is male and female together who reflect the image of God, not just the male. God is neither male nor female, but the characteristics of both sexes are incorporated in his person. This is what reason would expect revelation to disclose anyway. It is as impossible to imagine that God could create something that was not already part of himself as to imagine that a human painter or poet could create something that was not already part of themselves.

That God is not male is clearly reflected in the Gospels' picture of Jesus Christ. The four Gospel writers attach absolutely no significance to the fact that God incarnated himself in a male. Their only concern is that God became human. Their picture of

Jesus is that of a full human person incorporating so-called female characteristics, like compassion and tearfulness, and so-called male characteristics, like courage and strength. One of the most remarkable things about Jesus' friendships is that, contrary to strict Jewish rules and customs, he had a circle of close female as well as male intimates.

It is *human* personality — male and female — that reflects the image of God in us, not maleness or femaleness.

14 Midnight ascent

PAIN AND SUFFERING

Babies are born deformed, lightning strikes a golfer out on the fairway, an earthquake devastates a village, napalm bombs melt the flesh of war's innocent bystanders, a friend dies a torturous death from cancer. These are just some examples of the suffering that wrenches in us the cry: Why God, why? A Christianity which shirks the problem of pain and suffering does not deserve the name.

'God's in his heaven, all's right with the world' is not a Christian sentiment. Christianity certainly says God is in heaven, but it also says that 'a lot's *wrong* with the world'. Real Christianity should not be confused with those sweet poisons which tell of a dewy-eyed Christ and a fairy-floss world. Real Christianity seeks to find a way through . . . by journeying into the dark tragedy of suffering, not by running away from it. Its symbol is the cross Christ died on, a symbol of suffering. It knows that the problem of suffering, especially unjust suffering, is the only substantial objection to the truth of its reality map.

In fact the problem of unjust suffering is one of the central themes of the Bible. Not only is the Book of Job a part of the Christian revelation and one of the finest pieces of literature ever written; it is also one of the most profound explorations of the tension between divine love and human suffering one could ever read.

Before we take the Christian reality map in our hands and explore the region of human suffering, we must make an important distinction. We need to distinguish between people for whom suffering poses a great obstacle to Christian belief and commitment, and those for whom the problem of suffering is just an excuse for avoiding God.

I once had a neighbour who was extremely cautious about discussing religion. On the one occasion we began to discuss the subject deeply, he immediately threw up the problem of suffering. As a boy he had lived in Europe and experienced the dislocations of the war with Nazism. He said he could never believe in a loving God because of Hitler's treatment of the Jews. As far as he was concerned, there was nothing more to say. He was not interested in theological explanations of suffering. The irony of rejecting God because of the mistreatment of a people whose history of suffering produced Job and Christ was totally lost on him.

Now I knew this man well enough to know that he lived a very private life in a tiny circle of family and friends. I also knew that he was a selfishly materialistic person, climbing a career ladder and successfully speculating in real estate on the side. Love for him was a word with little meaning beyond himself and his little circle of relations and friends. The theological problem of suffering was just his excuse for avoiding the God who would challenge his own self-centred life. He did not really care about human suffering at all.

This chapter is not written for people like him — they would not read it anyway — but for that vast number of sincere people who find suffering a genuine obstacle to Christian belief and commitment.

Suffering as a painful personal experience is different from the theoretical, theological problem. No one who has just learnt they have terminal cancer or lost a child through death wants theological explanations of their suffering. They want love — someone to weep with them, be with them, perhaps physically hold them and, at the very least, give a caring ear to their anguished cries of anger and despair. The depths of personal sorrow or grief are not the place for theological answers, but for practical Christian love.

But theological answers do have their place — in times when we are able to be rational and reflective. Without such answers, we have no grounds for believing that God does ultimately love his creation. This chapter is written for people who are not presently in the depths of personal suffering, and thus are able to spend a little time calmly considering the accuracy of the Christian reality map.

The real problem

To begin, we must clearly understand why suffering poses such a difficult obstacle to belief in God's love. Most human suffering derives from human action or inaction and cannot be attributed directly to God. We cannot put a precise percentage on this proportion, but ninety per cent may not be all that unreasonable. This figure would include all accidents due to human error, all war, almost all malnutrition and starvation, all shattered personal relationships, and all disease and ill health resulting from environmental pollution or unhealthy habits. As a race, human beings undeniably produce most of their own suffering. This fact is often overlooked in discussions about the problem.

But it by no means solves all our theological difficulties. These difficulties are:

(a) Why does God give us freedom to be so cruel to each other and destructive to ourselves?

(b) What about natural disasters like earthquakes, cyclones and tidal waves which seem to be directly attributable to God?

(c) Why do good people sometimes suffer a lot when wicked people do not suffer at all?

Christianity says that all suffering is a consequence of human rebellion against God. Our world is twisted and fractured because *we* are twisted and fractured. It is not so difficult to see the reasonableness of this explanation for the vast proportion of suffering we heap on our own heads, both individually and as a race. It is harder to see how we could be responsible for the suffering produced by natural disasters or the pain animals experience. In this chapter we will explore the easier side of the problem — suffering caused by ourselves. The next chapter will look at the more complex problem of suffering in nature itself.

Suppose a craftsman makes a strong sharp-pointed knife for cutting melons. Suppose also that he announced to the world, 'This is a melon knife; it must not be used for any other purpose than cutting melons'. But the craftsman's apprentice has an elder brother whom he hates because his parents unfairly favour him. The apprentice steals his master's melon knife and stabs his elder brother to death with it.

Now Christianity says that God is like the craftsman and we are like the apprentice. God made a good world, but he also made free creatures like us to live in it. (We explored this freedom when we discovered that the transcendent self is a moral vacuum which must be filled by its own choices.) Christianity says that through conscience God commands us all to do good not evil, but we have all abused our freedom and chosen evil.

We do not blame the craftsman for the murder committed using his knife. Used for the purpose for which it was made, the knife was good. It took a transcendent will to wield the knife as an instrument of murder and suffering. The apprentice's will was evil, not the knife. Similarly we cannot blame God for the suffering produced by our human will. It is our fault.

Two objections might be made to this answer. First, unlike the craftsman, God knows what is going on in our minds and he also has the power to stop acts like murder — so why doesn't he? This objection gains even more force if we think about the possibility of God intervening to prevent war or to force rich countries to share their food with the world's starving.

Second, if suffering is our own fault, why doesn't God ensure that evil people suffer the consequences of their own actions? Often it is some innocent person who suffers instead. Even the apprentice who murdered his elder brother is an innocent victim of someone else's evil: his parents unfairly favoured his elder brother. And why should the elder brother have been the murder victim? Was it his fault that his parents favoured him? Shouldn't they have been punished rather than he?

To the first objection — why doesn't God act? — Christianity says that God knows what he is doing. The amount of freedom he has given us is just the right amount to allow the growth of that 'communion in separateness' which he created us for — no more and no less. If God kept intervening, that freedom would be destroyed. We would not have moral freedom if, every time we were about to do evil, God stomped on us. In the biblical story of our fall into evil, Eve is able to doubt whether disobeying God will have disastrous or beneficial consequences for her. Such doubt is the condition of moral freedom (see Genesis chapter 3). Without it we would be like the children of over-protective parents: never allowed to grow up and never allowed to learn from experience, including mistakes.

Suffering is the price we pay for abusing our freedom. But we can learn from suffering. The craftsman's apprentice will be sent to gaol for his crime, but he still has the choice of amending his ways or continuing to commit evil. He can make things better for himself or worse.

The question of why God does not ensure evil people receive their just dessert is more difficult. Christianity answers this second objection in two ways.

We are part of each other

First it says that we must not make the mistake of thinking that God made individuals entirely separate from each other. As bodies, we are all joined together — we share a common origin and a common humanity. Each human body came out of a female womb impregnated by male seed. If we could trace these physical emanations back in time, we would discover that we all have a common bodily origin.

But we are also part of each other as self-conscious spirits too. Here we need to recall Eva Adamson and the monkey boy again. The monkey boy was physically but not psychically human. Like all human beings Eva only became a self-conscious spirit because she was part of a historical human community. It is a demonstrable fact that we are physically and spiritually created as part of each other — in and through the whole historical community of humanity.

This is what St Paul meant when he said that we are 'in Adam' (see Romans chapter 5). *Adam* is the Hebrew word meaning 'man' or 'human'. To be an individual human means to be in humanity itself — in St Paul's words, to be 'in Adam'. Christian revelation has known for centuries this truth, recently rediscovered by modern sociology and social pyschology. But Christian revelation knows more than this as well.

Christianity says that it is not just individual humans who are evil and twisted, but humanity itself. We know that many bacteria and viruses invade human bodies, passed from one body to another by such things as sneezing and uncleanliness. But the potency of these diseases depends upon the general condition of the host environment — the health of our bodies. With a good diet and plenty of exercise we may hardly notice the infections that constantly invade our bodies. But poor condition and an inadequate diet allows the infection to thrive and make us ill.

Christianity says that whole of humanity is infected by evil too. This is probably the most indisputable fact on the Christian reality map. Now that we have some idea about how we become human, we can begin to suggest how this happens. Christian revelation says that the first self-conscious humans, represented in the biblical creation story as Adam and Eve, used their freedom to rebel against God's rules. From this point on, every human being was made a self-conscious spirit through relationships with spirits who were themselves evil. (Here again we need to recall how Eva Adamson became a self-conscious human in chapter 3.)

Nowadays we recognize this truth when we say that all parents make mistakes and there is no such thing as a perfect parent. In more direct language, we recognize that in varying degrees all parents act selfishly and unlovingly towards their children — that all parents are evil. Some parents are very good and some parents are very bad, but it is relative — no parent is perfect.

Christianity goes further and says there is no such thing as a perfect human being — all of us have rebelled against God, parents or not. This is the meaning of that much maligned and misunderstood Christian teaching called *original sin*. Because we are made self-conscious spirits in and through relationships where none of us have been perfectly loved, we reproduce that same lack of love by becoming selfish and aggressive ourselves. The flaw is there before we are born and biases us towards evil. But each one of us individually chooses to do evil too. Evil infection is universal, but the degree of infection is environmental. A practical example will make all this clearer.

The craftsman's apprentice is not an especially extreme example of a person suffering from cruel circumstances. But the apprentice was a victim of his parents' evil favouritism. Had his parents loved both sons equally, he would not have felt such hatred for his brother. We sympathize with him because we know that, in the same circumstances, we would have felt similar hatred and perhaps become murderers also.

But we must not allow the circumstances to excuse his crime. Plenty of other boys have experienced similar circumstances without becoming murderers. They have run away from home, taken out their aggression in sport or hard work, or just knuckled under to make the best of a bad situation. What our sympathy tells us is that the parents were also responsible for the elder brother's murder. Their evil contributed to the circumstances that led to the knifing. The apprentice took the further step and actually committed the crime. Our sympathy with the apprentice's circumstances should tell us that we are as potentially evil as he is.

In evil, no less than physical and self-conscious life, we are all part of each other. Our sins do not end with our lives; they go down each generation that follows us. The suffering we bring down upon our own heads is also brought down upon our children and grandchildren. This is why Jesus Christ commended us not to judge each other. We do not know whether a person born into cruel circumstances, becoming a prostitute or a murderer, is worse at heart than a person born into gentle circumstances who flirts teasingly or cheats on tax. Social functioning demands that we deal more firmly with the prostitute or murderer, but God may see things quite differently.

As we saw in the case of Eva Adamson, circumstances produce our *me*, but moral choice is made by the *I* which can transcend the *me*. All that Christianity claims is that every *me* has been infected by the evil of humanity and every *I* has succumbed to that infection by its own moral choice. At heart, says Christianity, each one of us has become selfish and aggressive. Every marriage, every human community (including churches), every newspaper — indeed the whole history of our race — is proof of this claim. Only those who have never tried to be more than commonly decent, or never experienced the temptations to hate produced by war or social distinctions, could believe otherwise. Collectively and individually most of our suffering arises from our own evil choices.

When tears are wiped away

But we still have the problem that some people suffer more at the hands of collective human evil than others. One woman walking home from the movies is raped, one house in the street is burgled, one careless airline pilot flies his plane full of passengers into a mountain-side — there are hundreds of examples. Why does God allow these things? Explaining them as the result of collective human evil does not make them any fairer for the victims. Fairness demands that everyone suffers the consequences of their own evil — no more and no less.

Now Christianity says that this is exactly what God does. He gives fair reward and punishment to all. The twin belief within every person that good is different from evil and that evil deserves fair punishment is the strongest pointer reason gives for another stage along the Christian reality map. This is the nub of the second part of the answer to the problem of unjust suffering.

Christians are not Marxists or secularists blindly believing in nothing beyond the ordinary everyday world. Christianity says that the self in us, which already partly transcends the space-time world, was made to live forever with God in heaven. Most women are prepared to endure several hours of pain for the joy of giving birth to a child. Compared to the joy of heaven, any suffering we may experience in this life is nothing. Compared to eternity, our earthly life will look briefer than a millisecond looks to us now. Even the worst human suffering will seem like the pain involved in removing a small splinter from one's finger.

The comparison is not strictly valid because eternity is timeless, not just the endless extension of time, but the point is the same. When we say that time heals suffering, we mean that forgetfulness of past suffering makes life bearable or even happy again. But we never *fully* forget past suffering. However joyful a woman's child has made her, she never totally forgets the pain she went through. But in heaven all memory of past suffering is *totally* erased. The Bible says it poetically: 'God will wipe away every tear from their eyes' (Revelation 21:4). Heaven is not just quantitatively different from the everyday life-world, but qualitatively different.

As I wrote this last paragraph I became aware of the coldness of the answer, even though I am convinced it is true. I thought of young men in the prime of physical life being tortured to death in their enemies' war prisons, of two parents wordlessly weeping as a tiny white coffin is lowered into the freshly cut earth before them. What are words of explanation in the midst of such agony? Here is the place for weeping with those who weep — to resolve to do everything in one's power to eradicate such evils from the earth, to practically see that God's will is done on earth as in heaven.

I thought also of Christ suffering on the cross. Could we believe in any but such a suffering God? Even in the extremity of our agony, human suffering cries out for a hope not available in this life. It cries out for the redress of all injustice and the healing of all pain. If there is nothing to answer that cry, suffering is worse, not better. Christianity says that the cry will be answered by a God who knows the suffering of crucifixion. But Christianity must be proved by Christian compassion, not just explanations or doctrinaire assertions.

Finally we come to the most difficult problem of all: the problem of suffering in nature. Though it raises difficulties about fairness, we can see how evil rebellious human beings bring hurt to each other and themselves. But how can our rebellion against God fracture and twist nature too? How could *we* be the cause of such things as earthquakes, genetic deformity, viral diseases, cyclones and animal pain? Surely God must take direct blame for these! In the next chapter we shall explore the Christian answer to these piercing questions.

15

Midnight ascent

THE LOST UNIVERSE

Science is now religion's greatest ally for disclosing the incredible mystery of life in this present universe. The imaginative piece of science fiction of one generation becomes the scientific fact of the next. Modern astromoners now seriously theorize not just about previously undreamed wonders of this universe, but about universes altogether different from ours. They speak of such marvels as black holes out there in the world of space — probably burnt-out stars whose matter has imploded to such density they they are falling out of our universe like giant cosmic drain holes. If it were possible to remain alive after being sucked into a black hole (it isn't — you would be destroyed), scientists believe we would enter a world where none of the present laws of physics applied. We would be in another reality.

Theology says we are already in a different reality from the one God first created for us. This present universe, with its seeming futility, pain and suffering, is not what God intended for us at all. Theology says there are enough traces of the old universe left in us for us to know the truth of this claim. It claims the natural universe has gone wrong because we have gone wrong.

There was a time when it was a little easier for theology to explain these things. That was in the days before people started to forget what an amazing mystery it is to be a self-conscious, knowing person. When people see that they themselves are 'holes in their universe', it is much easier to imagine the existence of other universes. But modern science is beginning to remind us of these things again.

We know that if a vital component fails in a human creation, say in a jet engine or a computer control system, the whole apparatus will malfunction. If the current theories about black holes prove accurate, then on the cosmic scale it appears that, when a star ceases to function in this universe, it may eventually fall into another universe.

Paradise lost

When we put these two pictures together, we can begin to get some idea of what Christianity says has happened to us and our universe. Theology says God made the first humans in a universe of perfect harmony and beauty and that all the successive generations, ourselves included, have emanated from them.

Perhaps the myths of a past golden age, which every civilization seems to possess, are some kind of genetic memory of this era. Theology says that every level of being had its place in this universe, not in disjuncture or at the expense of pain and suffering, but in harmonious unity. In their bodies human beings were part of the whole natural universe. In their transcendent spirits they were made like God, with the power of divine-like dominion over the rest of their world. They were meant to rule their universe with perfect love, maintaining the harmony and beauty God had given it.

So that they could really love, God made humans free to accept or reject him. They did reject God and, when they fell from perfection, their whole universe fell with them. Because they were the pinnacle of nature, created as the vital link between nature and God, when evil entered them it was like dropping black dye on to the surface of a beaker of clear water. Everything was suddenly infused with a dark cloud of horror.

The source of this theological explanation is the biblical stories of creation and the human fall into evil. Theology does not treat these stories as historically true (in the modern sense), but as theologically true. In a moment we will see that the explanation is not just wild speculation, but a revelation which accords with the actual facts of our present experience. But first a brief summary.

The biblical stories say that, before the fall into evil, Adam and Eve lived in a garden paradise. They were naked and had dominion over nature. They and all the animals were vegetarians. They enjoyed a close relationship of communion in separateness with God. But one thing was forbidden: they were not to eat of the fruit of the tree of knowledge of good and evil. (We will explore the meaning of this strange symbol in the next chapter.) God said death would be the penalty for disobedience.

But when they disobeyed and ate the fruit, a number of things happened. Physical death did not immediately occur, as a superficial reading of the story might lead us to expect. Death occurred in their relationship with each level of being.

Their close communion with God ceased (the *I* to *I* relationship). They were inwardly torn by guilt and fear (the *I* to *me* relationship). They experienced a new destructive separateness from each other which included lies, betrayal and sexual shame (all *I* to *you* relationships). They appear to have become flesh-eaters, their dominion over nature diminished and what remained was characterized by labour, drudgery and pain: they became subject to biological death (all *I* to *it* relationships). Most significantly, they were totally excluded, not merely banned, from the garden paradise with its tree of life.

Obviously the description of Adam and Eve's fallen condition is a description of the reality we live in, the space-time world of everyday life. We all know that there is a lot wrong with this reality. We 'rise above' it sufficiently to complain, even blame God for its faults. In itself this suggests we are some kind of aliens aware of a better world — at least a world minus the faults in this one.

Yet one element of this theological picture seems to be contradicted by the discoveries of modern science. Science says that the 'natural' causes of pain and suffering — earthquakes, cyclones, disease, death etc. — were in the universe long before self-conscious humans came on to the scene. Thus how could a human fall into evil cause what was already there?

If theology insisted that the story of the fall was part of the history of this universe as it is now, its explanation could only be valid if the theory of evolution was false. Of course this is possible; some scientists do believe the theory is false. But as this appears less than likely, it is not a course that will be pursued here. In fact the biblical story specifically states that the fall took place in another reality — symbolized by the paradisial garden from which humanity is banished.

According to Christianity the reality we are now in is some kind of reversal of the harmonious universe, with evil creating disharmony at each level of its being. It says the Genesis revelation discloses an original universe related to this one somewhat like positive to negative, light to darkness, matter to anti-matter, intact to shattered . . . or, to use a more homely image, like the ordered design side to the tangled reverse side of a tapestry. But the reversed reality only came into being when human beings 'turned the switch' they were forbidden to turn.

Like the rest of us, scientists themselves are totally excluded from the original universe. Thus their evolutionary theories can only describe the good creation now reversed and fallen into evil — including the evil of time. Without time, the original creation would be totally in the present, with no past or future — something we can only dimly imagine at best. But in this 'in time', fallen reality, everything appears to have developed through slow successive stages. And because the fall into evil permeated the whole reality with pain and suffering, nature itself appears to be infected with evil from the beginning. Put crudely, we might say that what our scientsts are now describing for us is something like a movie film of the original creation, projected through a cracked time-lens.

Memory, imagination and reality

To fully illustrate that ours is a universe fallen from perfection into evil would take a book itself. But two examples will show how much sense this explanation makes of our present experience. First, time and death.

Deep within every human being is a profound 'No' to death. Death seems to mock our self-conscious lives. We feel death is an anomaly — it should not be there. Although they try to repress this feeling, secularists share it too. The biblical story of creation says that falling into evil meant falling into all the evils of this present reality, including time and death.

In *Part One* we saw that time is personal. Time is the dimension in which self-conscious persons (who know they grow old) measure their lives against the movement and change of the 'out there' world. If there were no self-conscious beings, time would not be time, just movement and change. Earlier we noted that Einstein has shown that time is relative to our position in the universe. If we could travel through space near to the speed of light, time — as measured by friends remaining on earth — would slow down.

But theology is not particularly interested in the

'how' and 'what', but in the 'why' of time. Whatever our position in the universe, time is always the measure of movement and change against the still centre of our self-consciousness. We 'rise above' movement and change, including the movement and change of our own bodies, in order to be conscious of time. Time is not just astronomical, mechanical or electrical; time is personal. In an immensely profound sense, time is a measure of the tragic existence of self-conscious spirits in this present universe.

Individuals experience pain and suffering in many different ways — with one exception. The exception is death. Death is the tragedy that eventually strikes us all. We are creatures able to 'stand back' and view the passing years dissolve the grounds of our own personal being — the process of ageing which, we know, will end in biological death. Time is a measure of mortality against immortality. St Paul calls death 'the last enemy'. We are creatures who seem to contain (or retain?) enough sense of eternity in some kind of still, self-conscious centre, to make life in a world of time and death tragic.

No biblical book explores this sense of tragedy more deeply than Ecclesiastes. Its author reminds us that, even if we attain the great wealth, fame and power that he has attained, nothing in this present reality finally satisfies us. He says that the best does not last, and even the best is never enough because 'God has put eternity into man's mind' (Ecclesiastes 3:11). The Christian reality map claims this tragedy exists because we called time and death on our own heads — by rebelling against the eternal Being who created us.

The second example of this universe's lost perfection also concerns our relationship with nature. We know that nature shows hostility to us through disease, earthquakes, drought and cyclones. But more recently we have discovered that we are hostile to nature too, destroying the harmony it retains by pollution and environmental rape.

In itself this double-sided evil suggests we are wrong creatures in a wrong world. How could nature throw up a being hostile to it? (This is the negative side of the argument against crude materialistic evolution, the religion of matter. The positive side of the argument was put in the question: How can the impersonal produce the personal?) According to the biblical story, the fall cast human beings into a new, evil relationship with nature. In the garden paradise Adam and Eve had dominion over nature. It is described as 'tending' the garden, not ruling destructively and exploitatively over it. But the story says that, after the fall into evil, this dominion diminished to mere traces of what it had been and they entered a world of man-nature hostility.

It is likely that magic is some kind of distorted memory of our lost powers. Magic falsely believes that mind and imagination can control nature without great effort or danger. This is why people who believe in magic never develop science: they try to invoke rain by dances or land fertility by mimetic, ritual sexual intercourse.

But the truth of the matter is that, in this present reality, whatever dominion we achieve over nature's hostility comes through enormous mental and muscular effort. The biblical story puts it poetically as 'the sweat of our brow'. We might think of the long, slow developments in surgery, agriculture, engineering and medicine. But even our greatest achievements remain puny in face of nature's essential hostility to our being. Each of us finally succumbs to that hostility in death.

Aliens and strangers

In our present universe there is a very strange relationship between human imagination and the 'out there' reality. Like some kind of half-aliens, we can imagine many things we cannot do in reality. Yet, with more strenuous imagination and great effort, we often become able to project our imagination into the 'out there' reality itself. Flight is a good example.

For centuries human beings dreamed of flying like the birds. Through much imagination and dangerous experiment we finally succeeded. Today we can fly higher and faster than birds. Yet flight remains hedged with danger. Only with great care and effort does aeronautical engineering allow us to briefly push nature's hostility aside, enabling us to fly through its constant threat to hurt or destroy us. It still takes enormous co-operative effort to build, fly and maintain our giant jet aircraft.

The more we understand how this universe works, the more we can do things we have always imagined we could do. Now we can fly through the air like birds, swim for hours under the ocean like fish, even travel to the moon. Why can we imagine so many things? Why can we imagine things it seems we shall never be able to do, like travel backwards and forwards in time, or live forever? Why is the universe such a strange mixture of beauty and harmony, ugly destruction and chaos? We seem such strange creatures to ourselves. We even find it strange that we should seem strange to ourselves. Christianity says we *are* strangers. We have lost our true home and our true powers.

Objections

It will be objected that, although the Christian explanation of natural evil makes good sense, it is palpably unfair. Why should the whole human race suffer the consequences of our progenitors' fall into evil? And why should innocent animals suffer too? Christianity answers these objections in three ways.

First, we are made as part of a whole. We have already seen that we only become individually human as part of humanity. Nature also is one totality. Our bodies are part and parcel of the same material universe we share with the other animals. Presumably God could have made both us and nature differently, but this must have been the best way, otherwise God would not have done it. Because we are the spiritual beings for whom the universe was made, our evil fall took our whole reality with it.

Second, Christianity says we have each repeated the original rebellion. We stand guilty individually and together as a race. Which of us would claim to love God perfectly? Some of us do not even bother to try. In the biblical story Adam, as we saw, means human. This is not an insignificant detail. Its intention is to say that each of us is Adam, that Adam's story is *our* personal story as well as the story of humanity. We are responsible for all suffering and pain.

But the third answer is the most important. Christianity says God began the process to restore our fallen reality before it even fell. Human restoration is the centre of this process; human beings caused the need for it in the first place. But it includes the whole of nature too — everything, past, present and future. This restoration will more than compensate for the sufferings of this present reality. To translate St Paul idiomatically:

> *I consider that the sufferings we now endure bear no comparison with the glory that is going to be revealed to us. All of creation waits with eager longing for God to restore his children. For creation was made the victim of frustration, not of its own will, but by the will of him who subjected it in hope; because the universe itself will one day be set free from its slavery to decay and share the glorious freedom of the children of God. Up to the present we know that the whole created universe groans in all its parts with pain like the pain of childbirth* (Romans 8:18-22).

Shortly we will explore the Christian reality map's description of this restoration process — what it is, how it works and how we become part of it. But in the next chapter we must briefly examine what is wrong with us. Until we know this, we shall never understand how God can begin to reverse evil in us or in nature as a whole.

16

Treading the edge

BETWEEN HEAVEN AND HELL

Pantheists say the solution to the problem of pain and suffering is elimination of the self which feels pain and suffering. This is an ostrich solution. We cannot bury our heads in the sands of mystic flight from everyday life. Even to meditate one must eat, and to eat we must work — or someone else must work for us. Christianity says the cause of human tragedy is not ego but wilful, immoral ego. What needs to be eliminated is not the self, but the sinful self which rebels against God.

But how often one hears the Christian word 'sin' reduced to this sort of parody: 'We're good Christians — we don't smoke, drink or gamble'. And if not this triune of trivia, then sex. Paul the Apostle says sin brought death into the world. The whole Christian revelation agrees. But the word 'death' means the death we explored in the last chapter — the fractured harmony between every level of being — of which biological death is only a symptom. What a monstrous God people must believe in who think this death was caused by smoking, drinking and gambling . . . or illicit sex!

Not far to the north of Australia there is a fishing tribe recently converted to Christianity from animism. Without fish the tribe would perish. If a member of the tribe is caught committing adultery, he is forbidden to receive the sacraments in church for three months. But failing to lend your outboard motor to a fisherman friend whose own motor has broken down carries a stiffer penalty — six months exclusion from the sacraments. Sins of the mind and power are treated more severely than sins of the flesh and weakness. Tribal simplicity has got nearer to the truth about sin than more 'civilized' Christianity. Was Hitler a great sinner because he had a mistress? This rhetorical question is not meant to deny sexual sin, but may put it in proportion.

But what is this 'sin' which Christianity says brings death — death with its big biblical meaning?

The cause of it all

We have called this sin rebellion against God, but we did not say what this actually means. In the biblical story the rebellion is symbolized by eating forbidden fruit — not Adam's apple, as popular belief says, but the forbidden fruit of the tree of the knowledge of good and evil. A simple reading of the story might lead us to think that eating fruit from this tree would produce an intellectual knowledge about the difference between good and evil. But Adam and Eve had this kind of knowledge already. They knew that good meant obeying God and abstaining from the fruit, evil meant disobeying and partaking. The whole story seems silly, with all this business about God forbidding them eat a piece of fruit — like a child's tease. Only the total context reveals the story's profound meaning.

To understand the forbidden fruit we must first erase our usual sense of the word 'know'. A little further on, the story says Adam *knew* his wife Eve and she conceived and bore a son. 'Know' means something active and personal, like making sexual love, not abstract and impersonal. It is more like the way a medieval apprentice came to know how to paint and sculpt, than the abstract theory taught in modern university art schools. For Adam and Eve, knowing good and evil meant *doing* good and evil — deciding good and evil for oneself, without reference to God. It is like the modern relativist who claims there is no real right or wrong, just what you decide for yourself.

Now if we are to have real freedom in relation to God, we must be able to doubt him — to doubt whether reality is really like he says it is, or not. A practical example will make this point clearer. As a young high-school student I used to doubt my mother's ability to read the vagaries of Australia's east coast weather. 'Take an umbrella; it will rain this afternoon', she would say as I set out for school.

'No,' I would reply, asserting my adolescent independence, 'it's hot and sunny. It won't rain today.' But rain it nearly always did. I would arrive home soaked and shivering, invariably catching a cold for my folly.

The biblical story says God told Adam and Eve that eating the forbidden fruit would bring death, but they doubted. According to the story, Eve began to question the reality of the predicted consequences. She wondered whether God really cared about them or whether he was hiding something from them. Maybe, she thought, if we eat the forbidden fruit we shall not die, but become self-sufficient and all powerful like God himself.

This was the doubt which spawned the desire that caused the fall into evil — the desire of Adam and Eve to be their own God. There was nothing 'wrong' with the *doubt* — it was freedom's condition. But the desire to be God was the beginning of evil and the act of eating was its completion.

Sin, Christianity says, is the heart of the human problem. We do not know who we are, why we are here or how we are meant to live because we have turned our backs on God. The story of Adam is the human story, our story. We have each said 'No' to God — said 'No' to the One who gives ultimate meaning to every little meaning. *That* is what sin is — saying 'No' to God. Every other sin and evil is just a symptom of the real sin.

Strange as this claim may at first seem, there is probably nothing contemporary human beings need more than to rediscover a sense of sin. Without it, we will probably destroy life on this planet quite soon. But not before we have first destroyed most human relationships. It is not that modern people do not believe in sin. They do — in other people's sin and in 'the system's' sin, but not in their own sin. What is most needed is exactly what is missing — a profound sense of one's own sin and potential for destructive evil.

Christianity agrees that there is sin in others and in the social system too (after all it is a human creation), but it also says there is sin in you and me. Until Marxists learn this Christian truth, they will continue to be as evil as, or worse than, the corrupt capitalists and capitalism they want to overthrow. And until Western secularists learn about personal sin, they will never understand how their selfish greed causes world poverty, why their marriages are collapsing, or why their cities are beginning to teem with violence — to name just a few pertinent examples.

Loss of the sense of personal sin has gone hand in glove with loss of the sense of God. How can anyone see their own evil, except through the eyes of One who sees through the rationalizations of their own selfishness? There can be no peace or love if each always thinks the other is to blame. The more we turn our backs on God, the less we shall understand what is really wrong with us and our world.

Living without a core

It is no accident that modern relativists believe that they are God themselves and that all life is absurd and meaningless. In the biblical story that is what Adam and Eve found. Without God at the centre, life became meaningless. They had desired self-divinity — to be the source and ground of their own being and morality. Instead they discovered the truth of their dependence upon God, their created creatureliness. Once we sever the relationship for which we were made, there is nothing left but the tragic vision Adam and Eve saw — a vision of their own frailty and ultimate 'aloneness' in a world of matter and time without God.

According to Christianity, sin brought all human

tragedy, not just the interior tragedy of lost identity. In the last chapter we saw that most human suffering derives from evil human behaviour. It derives from selfishness, described in Christian terms as the willing of one's own self above God and above fellow human beings. This is so whether that selfishness shatters face-to-face relationships (like marriage, friendships or business partnerships), or whether it is group selfishness shattering social relationships (like war, racism and poverty). When the centre fails, all the spokes begin to give and twist.

The biblical story mirrors this problem. After the fall from God, Adam and Eve begin to lie and betray each other, they become locked in personal and sexual hostility (sexism), and their eldest son murders his younger brother. The story is a profound explanation of the ills of humanity. How sad it is to see modern university students treating this story as mere fairy-tale, or feminists reducing its symbols to nothing but Freudian sexual meaning. It may not be history, but it is not fairy-tale. And it is certainly not Freudian mythology. But the story does explain sexism — as one of the evils deriving from the sin of men and women in rebellion against God.

The story of Adam and Eve also attributes 'natural' suffering to human sin. It says that the dislocations in the natural environment also stem from the rift with God. Three telling examples stand for the whole of 'natural' suffering. First, there is the pain of childbirth, that cruel irony of screaming despair and joy that marks the beginning of us all. Second is the hostility of nature — all those earthquakes, droughts and cyclones which spread the fear of nature and the doubt of God into every fibre of our being. Third is biological death itself. In the words of God to Adam: 'dust you are and to dust you shall return'. Even if a loving family and pleasant circumstances make us see the world rose-coloured, this dark enemy casts a long shadow that finally traps all its prey.

Of course although the fall into evil resulted from the abuse of human freedom, God must have known it was going to happen, for he knows the future as well as the past and present. Therefore it might be objected: Why did he create us and our world at all? The answer, part of which was given in the last chapter, is threefold:

(a) because God had already planned the solution to the human tragedy before it occurred, a solution which retained human freedom;

(b) because God knew that the outcome to this solution would make all human suffering worthwhile; and

(c) because God knew that even through suffering, perhaps only through suffering, could humanity become what he intended it to be.

The next two chapters will show the way from our rebellion's darkness back to the light of God, where this present life becomes a journey, not a game or an accident. But before we leave the darkness behind, we must heed the Christian map's warning of a midnight descent, of a dark terror worse than worldly suffering.

Death and nothingness

Nowhere does Christianity conflict more with so-called modern ideas than about death. Christianity says that the transcendent self, our spiritual personality, was made to live eternally. We have seen tiny glimmers of eternity in it as we have explored its life here in the world. But these glimmers are only sparks of the glory God intended it to be.

Modern secularists do not face death. But when death makes itself unavoidably obtrusive, you will hear their shallow phantasies. At funerals secularists can often be heard to say such things as, 'Oh well, poor Grandpa is better off now; he was so lonely (or sick)'. They do not mean Grandpa is better off because he is with God in heaven, where he really would be better off. Secularists do not really believe in heaven, though they tend to have traditional religious funerals, just in case. They seem to mean Grandpa is better off because he is nothing — non-existent, evaporated from being.

When the clergy who conduct these funerals hear such talk, it must take every last ounce of compassion for the bereaved to prevent them from openly questioning it. For what if Grandpa, however great his suffering, has really gone from the frying pan into the fire? Wouldn't it be better to stay in the frying pan while there was a chance of learning how to avoid the fire? Failing to see the mystery of life, secularists approach the greater mystery of death with the simple-mindedness of idiocy. They reject Christianity because they think it calls for a mindless leap of faith. But without deep thought, and wilfully blind to the glimmers of eternity within their own being, they punt on the half-comfort that death is nothingness — like going to sleep. But even sleep can be plagued with nightmares, and we do wake up.

Christians can agree with secularists this far: if death is nothingness then, once you are in it, there is nothing to fear. Nothingness is quite horrible to contemplate now while we are still something — like the last foothold before falling into a bottomless pit. But a dreamless eternal sleep could not be bad or good . . . and this is just the trouble.

What if we let ourselves *needlessly* fall into nothing when we had the possibility of becoming more real and more joyful than we had ever been, even in the best moment of our worldly lives? And worse, what if death is not nothing, but a reality filled with more suffering than life? If they discount this possibility, secularists have put their faith in a belief held by a tiny minority of humankind.

Hitler and Christ

Not so curiously, reason itself provides clear pointers to some kind of after-death damnation. Reason knows that good is different from evil, however difficult it may be to explain. But reason also knows that the scales of justice do not balance in this life. Therefore if good is the ultimate victor over evil, there must be redress in another life.

This argument has more force if we imagine a situation like the following. Suppose Hitler had been captured at the end of the Second World War. What could we have done with him to compensate for the abject misery he wreaked on millions of Jews? Would years of meticulously planned torture have been enough? Or would that merely add evil to evil, drenching those who performed and permitted it with the same demonic filth? But where is the triumph of good if people like Hitler forever escape the consequences of their almost unbelievable evil? And if God is to be the torturer, would not he begrime himself with evil upon evil too? Reason suggests a crying need for balancing the scales of justice, but how?

Before we answer this question, we must not allow the example of Hitler and his like to divert us from our own sins. St Paul is right when he says the true fear of death is not nothingness, but sin — and, by implication, God's judgment of sin. That each of us will individually face the judgment of God upon our sins is clearly disclosed by Christian revelation. The Bible says that we know this to be true even without the benefit of revelation; it is written into our being (Romans 2: 14-16). From Christianity's point of view, denial of this knowledge is just another example of escapist secular phantasies.

Psycho-analysis provides some clues to what judgment may be like. Psycho-analysts tell us that nothing we ever experience or do is lost to memory, not even the experiences of early childhood. Now we know that most of what we have experienced and done in life is lost to conscious recall, so what does psycho-analysis mean? It means that nothing is ever lost to the *unconscious* mind, never lost to that vast bulk of consciousness which remains submerged beneath the surface of moment to moment consciousness. Only in dreams or psycho-analysis itself does this submerged memory emerge. In dreams we all experience memory-recall which we are incapable of performing during waking consciousness. Sometimes moderate alcoholic intoxication produces a similar, but fainter, effect. A personal example will help to describe the phenomenon.

In my teens I was forced, against my real will, to end a torrid romantic relationship. Driven by repressed passion, I tried for years to keep alive the memory of what the girl I loved looked like. I knew she was very pretty, but my conscious memory could only picture the vaguest outlines of her face. As might be expected, I would often dream about her and, in those dreams, she was as real as the days when we were going out together — even to the finest detail of her features. Yet on waking all I could remember was that she was very real in the dream, but just as vague as ever to my waking memory. But my unconscious memory had forgotten nothing. Next time you dream about someone important in your past, try comparing your memory of the dream experience of them with what you can actually picture with the conscious, waking memory. I think you will find your experience is similar to mine.

Speaking of God's judgment, Jesus Christ said these frightening words:

> *I tell you, on the day of judgment men will render account for every idle word they utter* (Matthew 12:36).

In recent times, until psycho-analysis rediscovered the unity of human consciousness with every past experience and deed trailing after everyday consciousness like a cosmic tail behind a comet, Christ's words seemed almost ridiculous. But Christianity has always insisted on the unity of the self: past, present and future. That is why it says that every moral action is either pushing us farther from God into unreality, or drawing us nearer to him with fuller reality. Life is a journey towards God or away from him. We are already ascending deeper into heaven or descending deeper into hell. Of course what we are talking about is the journey of the spiritual personality, not some mythical physical journey up into the sky or down below the earth's crust.

Psycho-analysis also tells us that the things we find hardest to recall are painful experiences, experiences which have hurt our personalities. To avoid suffering, we have pushed them into the unconscious, beyond recall. Take people's failure to remember the horrific last moments of a severe motor car accident. In this case amnesia is an obvious blessing. But mental disorder can arise from repressing hurts that need resolution. Repressing such memories is like trying to dam a flood; the pressure has to break through somewhere, often in distortions which have little obvious connection with the real trouble's flow. Usually the real trouble is permeated with guilt — some necessary and some the result of other people's false judgments, but mostly a bit of both. Psycho-analysts are trained to help patients recall unconscious memories and resolve false guilt, for example the guilt deriving from failure to meet a parent's unreasonable expectations. But they are powerless before true guilt, guilt resulting from actual sins. Unless the analyst is able to point his or her patient to divine forgiveness, there is little hope of a full cure.

Fading without fading away

We can now try to picture judgment and damnation, trying also to answer the question about Hitler. But we must remember that this terrible horror is on the Christian reality map as a warning. God does not want anyone to experience damnation, not even Hitler. God wants us all to be restored to that 'communion in separateness' with him for which we were made. We shall soon see how God's love has made that possible. But we can still persist in rebellion. God still leaves us free to accept or reject his new solution. He never forces us to love him, for without freedom real love is impossible. But if we persist in rebellion to death, we shall discover that we have freely damned ourselves.

Because judgment takes place in heaven, we can only think of it in pictures. Two of the pictures Jesus Christ used were the sorting of sheep from goats and wheat from weeds. When he talked about damnation, he used picture images of loneliness and despair — like 'being cast into outer darkness' and 'weeping and gnashing of teeth'. The following imaginative construction reflects the orthodox reality map.

After biological death, the persistent rebel's spiritual personality lives on and passes into the divine presence. God does nothing except to be himself — radiating with infinite love and goodness. But the rebel is nauseated with unimaginable horror. His own self, not God, is the source of that horror. For the first time ever, he sees what his moral choices have made him — not in comparison with other evil humans, but in comparison with perfect goodness. It is worse than a nightmare where one is transported into the centre of a formal church-wedding, dressed in rags and covered with filth and dung. Every recess of the personality stands naked and revealed before God — including all secrets previously concealed in shame from others, and all secrets kept hidden from oneself in the unconscious. Thousand upon thousand of a lifetime's acts of hate, greed, pettiness, gossip, jealousy — the whole catalogue of selfishness — glare like pathological cancers before an X-ray.

Of course nothing shows except the evil for which the rebel was personally and individually responsible. But still the experience is infinitely worse than a severely burnt person seeing their charred body in a mirror for the first time. God continues to do nothing except to be himself. But this is what the rebel cannot bear. He cannot bear to remain an instant in the presence of perfect love and goodness, in the presence of the One with whom he was made to find his fulfilment. All he feels is separateness without loving communion. He wants to run as far away as possible from the uncreated Being who fills all. But the desire to flee only produces the sensation of fading into unreality — never totally fading away, always haunted by God's quiet presence.

We can see now how God can remain perfect love and goodness, but still balance the scales of justice. Damnation is *self* damnation. It is the wish to live as one's own God come true — the self-centred self turning in its own little circle, all alone. The joke that says hell will be all right because all my friends will be there too is not true.

No Christian likes to speak or write about the

region called damnation. But it is there on the Christian reality map. To remain silent would be dishonest. Yet no Christian must ever use the fear of it to persuade others to return to God. Only cringing submission, not love, results from fear. Nothing but God's love can turn a rebellious person back to him. The rebel will rightly reject any attempt to manipulate the direction of his life through fear. He will say we have only invented the story about damnation to scare him. *Damnation* is a word Christians should label 'for personal use only'. A Christian should put the fear of damnation into one person alone — his or her self. Having done that, Christians will be able to speak quietly about damnation, without using it manipulatively.

What happens to a rebel self after the experience just described is a matter orthodox maps differ about. Some say the damned remain eternally fixed in their contorted aloneness. Other maps say that the experience brings most rebels to their senses and that, after appropriate preparation, they become ready to accept God's solution to their fall into evil. But those who still persist in asserting their will against God are allowed to do so, remaining damned eternally. Still other maps say that after the scales of justice have been fully balanced, the rebel self is allowed to fade away completely.

These differences have arisen because the Christian revelation is not particularly clear about the details of damnation. That is to be expected; it is really interested in God's solution, not in damnation. In the light of these differences I think it is only fair that I should give my own opinion. But I stress it is my own opinion and should not carry the weight of all those things which *are* clearly drawn on the Christian reality map.

Because I know the depth of my own evil will, I can readily accept the need for some kind of damnation. But I am in no position to judge anyone else — not even Stalin or Hitler. Because he is perfect love, I cannot believe God would allow any of his creatures to exist in a state of eternal damnation. Yet, knowing my own wilfulness, I can believe that it is possible for someone to eternally persist in self-assertion, remaining unwilling to love and be loved. Thus I presume that God eventually allows such people to fall into uncreation, into nothingness.

It is the Christian reality map itself, not a private opinion, which says that what God really wants is for all of us to return to a loving relationship with him. It is time we left the horrors of darkness behind and turned to the centre of Christianity.

17 From damnation to laughter

GOD IN CHRIST

Long ago it was thought nature was constructed from four basic elements: earth, air, water and fire. But making sense of nature has taken us far beyond such simplicity. Now we speak of sub-, or even sub, sub-atomic particles. Nature is so complex we never expect to fully fathom its mysteries. Therefore it should not surprise us that when we move to the only reality that is 'above' nature, personality, we should encounter complexity too.

In *Part One* we explored a little of this complexity. We saw that human personality arises from a trinity of relationships: I, me and you. Our journey has taken us far beyond the caricature of God as the old bearded man who sits on a cloud in the sky. But what kind of person is God? Is he like a super-human person, or is divine personality more complex than human personality?

Part of the answer to this question embarrasses Christians. God, they say, has three complete personalities in one person. He is a tri-unity or trinity. God is I-me-you in himself — he is complete in himself; he does not need anyone else to make him a person. This is because there are three I-me-you personalities in God. Yet he is still only one person. Christianity finds tri-unity embarrassing because it contradicts ordinary reason. It is the same as saying one equals three and three equals one.

If Christianity was a religion merely invented by human imagination, we would not expect to discover this embarrassing illogicality at the centre of its belief about God. But Christians did not make up this belief; their experience of God forced it on them. Science faces a similar embarrassment with the nature of light. In some circumstances physicists have to assume that light is material — a stream of particles. In others, they have to assume it is non-material — a wave-length. But the assumptions are contradictory; it cannot be both. Perhaps one day soon a scientific genius will resolve the dilemma, but meanwhile physicists can only account for their actual experience of light by a self-contradictory theory. Reality itself forces it upon them.

We can never expect to define or explain God. If we could explain him, we would be greater than him, which is silly. But this is what many so-called rationalists demand, which is sillier still. Even in heaven, God's inner nature will remain mysterious to us; how could it ever be otherwise? Thus is is not really surprising that when Christianity came to put its deepest experiences of God into words, those words expressed a rational contradiction we call the Trinity. Being a highly rational religion, Christianity would have liked something tidier, but experience would not allow it. Christianity is sufficiently rational to know the limitations of finite reason, but Christianity would be suspicious if its deepest experience of God did not end with mystery.

The highest level of personality

All the men and women who first knew Jesus Christ were Jews, and therefore strict monotheists. For centuries Judaism had firmly held to belief in one God in the midst of all the crudities of pagan polytheism. But the more these Jewish disciples experienced Jesus — his teaching, his moral life, his supernormal powers — the more convinced they became that nothing explained him except the theory that he was God in human flesh and personality. Two experiences finally convinced them beyond doubt. First, that after being dead for three days, they saw him risen to life again. Second, just as Jesus had predicted (or promised) after he had finally vanished from the everyday reality, they had an experience of the closeness of God such as they had never experienced before. This was an intensely mystical experience, a sense that God's personality somehow came inside their own personalities. Jesus had called it 'the coming of the Holy Spirit'.

For a century or so Christians did not even begin to put their new experience of God into explanatory words. They retained strict monotheism like the Jews, but they also worshipped Jesus and exulted in the mystical presence of God as Holy Spirit — just as most of humanity through the ages has similarly enjoyed and experienced light without ever bothering to try and explain it.

But it was not long before some great Christian minds began to suspect illogicality. If Jesus was God and the Holy Spirit is God, then, they thought, God must appear in three guises for he is the Creator too. That seemed logical enough: one God who appears in three ways.

But other great Christian minds did not think this really accounted for the total experience of God. For example, Jesus prayed to God. Was he just talking to himself? It did not seem so! And, put a little crudely, who was looking after the universe when God was in human flesh and personality as Jesus? And how could God be in his own heaven-reality and here in our personalities as the Holy Spirit at the same time? After a couple of centuries of very hot debate, and some almost unpardonable behaviour, orthodoxy said only the Trinity map could contain the facts of experience, even though it contradicted normal reason. God, it said, is three persons — Father, Son and Holy Spirit — in one God.

Accepting the Trinity was an embarrassing assault on normal human reason, but in some ways it was to be expected, not just because the Trinity map retains a sense of God's mystery, but because it also makes sense of a higher level of personality. In each one of us, personality is a trinity: the I-me-you relationship. Therefore we should not be at all surprised to discover that the personality from which we are derived is also a trinity of relationships.

We however are never complete in ourselves. As the comparison between Eva Adamson and the monkey boy showed, we need others (or an other) to become a person. God does not need anyone — he is three complete persons in himself. If this were not the case, it would make no sense to say that God is love. Love is a relationship *between* persons. Christianity says love is the essence of God's nature, because from eternity to eternity love is passing back and forth between the persons of the Trinity.

Jews and Muslims do not accept the Trinity. They have never believed in the divinity of Christ. They seem to think that Christianity has compromised the higher logic of monotheism with the cruder logic of polytheism. But Christians insist that they are strict monotheists. They admit that pagan polytheists may have guessed a half-truth, like the men who sewed bird feathers to their arms had some idea that human beings could fly if they tried hard enough. But there are not many gods, as the polytheists thought, but three persons in one God.

Christianity says that personality in God is more complicated than Jews and Muslims think. Doesn't the threefold relationship which produces human personality suggest a higher, more complex set of relations within divine personality? Christianity claims that Jesus Christ was the fullest uncovering of God's nature available to human beings. It does not say Jews and Muslims think of God incorrectly, but inadequately. It asks Jews to think again about Jesus and the claim that he really was the expected Messiah. It asks Muslims to seriously consider whether Jesus was really a lesser person than Muhammad. Certainly no one, not even Muslims themselves, claim that Muhammad was morally perfect. But this is what Christianity claims about Jesus and no one has ever seriously challenged the claim. And how could God be love if he is just one, as Jews and Muslims say?

Love is a tough word

Love is the point where all this abstract theology becomes practical. Christians do not insist on God's tri-unity because they like playing around with words, but because of their experience of God's love. The difference between Christianity and the other high monotheistic religions is not theoretical; it is about the experience of God's love, and about the kind of moral life that experience should produce in us.

As he was being nailed to the cross, Jesus looked compassionately upon those executing this grisly task and prayed, 'Father forgive them for they know not what they do'. It is hard to think of a greater example of human love than this. Ordinary people fume with murderous thoughts when someone pushes ahead of them in a rush hour queue or at the end of a trying day with their kids, not to mention the hate we harbour for our real enemies. If we gloss over our own evil depths we shall never understand the centre of Christianity, Christ's death. It was true Christian vision which said, 'Without Christ men would kill each other down to the last two men on earth'.

A popular misconception believes that being good is the way to restore our broken relationship with God. But trying to return to God by being good is like trying to give birth to yourself — it's impossible. Anyone who believes otherwise has never really tried to be good. What they call goodness is mere social respectability — conventional goodness. Conventional goodness hates real goodness.

The Pharisees epitomized socially respectable, 'Mr and Mrs Good Citizen' goodness and they hated Jesus. They hated him because his unconventional goodness exceeded their goodness. It included his love for prostitutes, lepers and traitors (the Jews who collected tax as agents of the Roman occupation). And they hated him because he put human need above religious rules — such as curing the sick on holy days, which forbad such expressions of compassion.

Christianity says that Jesus Christ had a perfect relationship with God because his love for God and humanity was perfect. A pregnant woman does not hope and pray for a baby with at least one leg and six fingers. She hopes and prays for a physically perfect baby, without any deformity at all. God wants perfection too. He wants perfect human spirits, without any moral deformity at all. If goodness is the way back to God, then we must see that Jesus Christ is the standard. We will have to be as good as Jesus, not merely better than average or Hitler. Real goodness prays 'Father forgive them' as it is being nailed to a cross. It says 'love your enemies', not 'give them a just tit-for-tat' as the Muslims say.

Every single person who has tried to be as good as Jesus has given up in disillusion. They discovered previously unimagined depths of demonic selfishness and aggression within themselves. Honest people know they could not have prayed Christ's prayer from the cross; they know how hard it is even to forgive their next-door neighbours for keeping them awake with the noise of a wild birthday party. Conventional goodness is a very thin membrane, fearfully stretched over a pit of human horrors. Really good people know the depths of their evil. That is why saints always say they are great sinners. It is not false modesty; they know they are great sinners, as does anybody who seeks great virtue.

Through the ages people who deeply cared about restoring their broken relationship with God knew a price had to be paid for wickedness. They tried everything: self-flagellation, animal sacrifice, fasts, pilgrimages, renunciation of wealth, hours of prayer or meditation. Some deluded souls even indulged in the horror of child sacrifice. But nothing gave lasting peace. Always they fell back into their old selfish ways and the need for another endless round of self-inflicted punishment or sacrifice.

Often their acts were half-crazed, but the sentiments were usually right. Even in ordinary human relationships, a price has to be paid for wickedness. Parents who fail to justly punish a child's misdemeanours will produce a self-centred brat, as much a menace to himself as others. No social order could survive where its courts forgave thieves, rapists and murderers without imposing a fair penalty. Of course loving parents and kind-hearted judges would like to forgive without punishment, but they know it does not work. We do not learn from mistakes which cost us nothing.

Christianity is the religion of divine forgiveness. It says there is nothing we ourselves can do to restore our broken relationship with God. Spiritually we are like shipwrecked sailors drifting helplessly at sea in a leaking life-boat; our only hope is rescue. But how can God forgive us? His love is so great he does not wish to add to the sufferings we have already pulled down upon our own heads. But he knows that in our present condition we could not come close to him without experiencing damnation. And if he forgives us without penalty, both he and we know that would turn us into spoilt children, without any real respect for goodness at all.

Christianity says that God had the solution to this dilemma within himself before he even created the universe. The centre of this solution is the death of Christ.

There is no hope for sailors shipwrecked in a gale unless kind and courageous rescuers risk their own lives out in the hostile elements. Perhaps God could have plucked us from the sea of evil by some kind of armchair miracle, but that would have destroyed our real freedom. Instead God chose an *inside* rescue. From eternity he had planned to unite the second person of his tri-unity with a man we now call Jesus Christ. God would go to the eye of the storm — would enter human history in and through the flesh and personality of Jesus Christ. Because evil had twisted and fractured humanity, God would start a new humanity. He was not going to abandon his creatures like some hapless potter smashing flawed firings into eternal oblivion. If we had gone wrong in and through each other (in Adam), then God was going to begin restoration in and through a new kind of human (in Christ). And if our self-inflicted suffering blinded our eyes to his love, God would show the depths of his love by suffering in and with the only perfect human being ever to live.

Christ's death is the bitterest irony in human history. We must never blame the Jews and Romans for it. *Humanity* crucified Christ. He died a death reserved for criminals and revolutionaries because he was too good for human beings to bear. Each one of us would have joined the mob and cried 'Crucify him' too. None of us can bear real goodness. We cannot even bear people who are better than us. That is why we have to destroy them with gossip and slander, however petty.

The same pride and false self-confidence which crucified Jesus has more recently announced that 'God is dead' because we do not need him anymore. This folly arose from the new material power science and technology gave us. But the more power we have, the more dangerous we become — as much to ourselves as others. How much safer it is if the man who holds his finger on the missile button believes in his own evil before God than if he does not. Of course it would be better still if there were no missile buttons at all, but that is pure idealism in the reality we have created here on earth.

Christ's death weighs upon the world as the ultimate judgment upon human sin. Grasping to become God ourselves, we would not let anything stand in our way, not even the 'murder' of God himself. But Christ's death was also the grounds for our forgiveness — that is the divine irony.

All Christians agree that, because Christ died, we can be forgiven. They do not agree about how this works — many theories have been offered — but they do agree that this was the centre of God's solution. Somehow the price for human wickedness was paid by God himself with the death of Christ. Perhaps we can think of it this way.

Suppose there is a husband who loves his wife with unfaltering affection. But he knows she is having an affair with another man. Coming home unexpectedly one afternoon, he discovers his wife and her lover in bed together. He is filled with grief but, such is his moral perception, he knows the futility of seeking angry revenge. He is quite prepared to talk things over, to forgive them both and to start again.

But the two lovers cannot bear this sensible attitude; they would have coped better with an angry scene. They hate him for what they call his simpering goodness which they interpret as weakness, not strength. Their hate wells up into physical attack and, together, they kill him. When the deed is done, their guilt proclaims that, if anyone deserved such treatment, it was they themselves. A terrible price has been paid for their wickedness by someone who did not deserve to pay it.

Now this is how Christians explain Christ's death. He paid the penalty we deserved. It was not just the penalty of a torturous physical death — many others have suffered that too. The real suffering of Christ is disclosed in the cry from the cross, 'My God, my God, why have you forsaken me?'

We do not properly understand that cry of desperation because we have never enjoyed a perfect relationship with God. But at that moment the human side of Christ, that spiritually perfect humanity, endured the 'God-forsakenness' of the dammed. At human hands, in a world of humanly-created evil, Christ suffered. He truly felt that God had abandoned him.

If that had been the end, then there would have been no Christianity — there would have been no more hope associated with the death of this perfect human than with the earlier death of the kindly, but sinful, Socrates. However noble the rescuer might be, if he perishes with those he came to save, tragedy is merely compounded. If there had been nothing more to the story than the martyrdom of a good man and a fine ethical teacher, Christianity would have perished with Jesus on the cross.

From fear to faith

In some Eastern Orthodox churches Easter Sunday worship begins with the congregation breaking into peals of laughter. Nothing could be more appropriate. 'The third day he rose again from the dead' is orthodoxy's summary of the divine act which turned unmitigated tragedy into triumph. To this day the truth of Christianity hinges on the truth of the resurrection of Christ from death. Some secularized Christians, lulled into conformity to a consciousness that phantasizes life and death as 'ordinary', try to explain the resurrection as the inspired revival of Christ's teaching. But if 'raised' merely equals 'inspired', then no rescue took place.

But it was not his ideas which overnight transformed Christ's grieving and terror-striken disciples into people who feared nothing and no one. They themselves had only one explanation — God had raised Christ to life and they had seen him *alive*.

Forty days after the resurrection, Christ vanished

from the everyday reality into heaven. Because the Bible says Jesus was assumed into a cloud, some people have claimed that Christians really do believe heaven is up in the sky. But his disciples knew their Old Testament well enough to realize that the glory of clouds had always symbolized the glory of God. This was simply God's way of saying that Jesus was now with him in heaven eternally.

If the event had taken place in the twentieth century, perhaps God would have dematerialized Jesus before the disciples' eyes. No doubt this would be an easier symbol for us, but not for fifth-century Christians, and probably not for thirtieth-century Christians either. (The idea that Christianity is an old religion about to perish from senility is another Western secularist phantasy. As a percentage of the total world population, Christianity gained more converts in the nineteenth and twentieth centuries than in any other period of its history. The decline of Christianity in modern Western society probably says more about the senility of that society than Christianity!)

According to Christianity, Christ's extraordinary resurrection will eventually seem so ordinary to us that death itself, if we are permitted to remember it at all, will seem fantastic. For Christ is simply the first shipwrecked sailor to reach shore. Writing about AD 55, St Paul explained the resurrection to Greek Christians like this: 'Christ has been raised from death as the guarantee that those who sleep in death will also be raised' (1 Corinthians 15:20).

Theology calls Jesus Christ the new Adam (the new human), because with him God began the process of reversing the fall into evil. The resurrection is the reversal of biological death. If we are to participate in this reversal, we must get out of the old humanity and into the new. This is such a drastic process that Jesus called it a new birth. But the resurrection of our own spiritual personalities, with all their evil reversed to love, will mark the end of our journey in time and space.

Modern medical science has discovered that, during each seven year period of this life, every cell in our bodies is replaced by a new cell. Yet through this remarkable transformation, we experience the continuity of personality, both conscious and unconscious. When the New Testament describes the resurrection of the dead, it seems to draw its evidence from the post-resurrection appearances of Christ. What these appearances reveal is probably more fascinating to minds exposed to modern science and science fiction than to minds in any previous era.

At first Jesus' disciples did not recognize him. (This is an embarrassing detail for those who want to dismiss the stories as fictional. An invented tale would almost certainly have described instant and certain recognition.) But conversation soon established Jesus' identity to them. This suggests continuity of personality with some kind of transformed physical existence. Also, unlike the preresurrected Christ, the post-resurrection Christ is not limited by the space-time reality. He is able to appear suddenly in a locked room and to disappear just as incredulously. In modern language, he seems to have the capacity to materialize and dematerialize at will. It is a new dominion over nature.

Christianity has always said that, when we fell into evil, we fell into death. In this present reality death is the only certainty which follows birth — it is built into our biochemical existence. Theology says that, whatever else our resurrection will be, we will be raised with new bodies. St Paul calls it a spiritual body. He contrasts it with the flesh and blood body 'which cannot inherit the kingdom of God'. It is our personalities which God will raise, but with a new body — not some wispy floating existence, but a transformed bodily existence.

It is not only our bodies which need transformation, but also our spiritual personalities. In fact, they are the main problem, as we saw in the last chapter. Christians are not supposed to sit around and wait for the resurrection, but to get on with the journey 'into God' here and now. In the final chapters we will explore this journey.

* * *

Countless books have been written on the resurrection of Christ and they can be purchased just about anywhere in the world. One of the best known was written by an author who originally set out to prove the belief was a superstition. But in the course of his research he found the evidence so convincing he became a Christian himself. The book he eventually published argues for the truth of the resurrection, but evaluates the opposing arguments as well.* This present book is not about the resurrection, but one or two comments should be made.

* Frank Morrison, 'Who Moved The Stone?' Faber Paperback, 1978. Originally published in 1930.

Historically speaking, the evidence for Jesus' resurrection is as strong as other ancient historical facts most people just take for granted. The head of the Ancient History department at one of the universities here in my own city of Sydney says: 'Given the historical evidence to hand, the most likely explanation of the events is the one given by the disciples — that Jesus rose from the dead'. Anyone can research the historical evidence for themselves — there is abundant material. Admittedly a resurrection is not a 'normal' historical event. No amount of historical evidence will convince anyone who already believes in the impossibility of resurrections. Belief or disbelief will depend on our total view of reality.

To someone who already experiences life as an incredible mystery, who is also amazed to be a creature which can imagine its own death, anything which has good supporting evidence will seem possible. If such a person has, on other grounds, also come to believe in the reality of God, they would naturally expect some kind of divine answer to the problem of death. This is a reasonable assumption, not a gullible response. But anyone still locked into the old mechanical view of nature, where even the space-time reality seems as ordinary as the end of one's nose, will rule out a resurrection by assumption — despite good evidence to the contrary.

There is also a moral dimension to belief in the resurrection. If someone does not wish to cease living for self and to start living in relationship with God, they will not want to be convinced of anything that might disturb their present way of life. Jesus knew this. That is why he said of persistent rebels, 'Neither will they be convinced if some one should rise from the dead' (Luke 16:31).

18

Daring to follow

FAITH AND BELIEF

A great Christian thinker (Soren Kierkegaard) once said, 'You cannot teach Christianity to another person'. He was right. Ultimately Christianity is a passionate personal commitment which can only be experienced, not taught.

Long ago it will have become obvious that one aim of this book is to uncover the grounds for belief in Christianity. But belief is not sufficient. The first Christians called themselves 'followers of the Way' — a name which expressed their experience of Christianity as a journey of the *whole* self, not just the mind. The split self is another tragic distortion produced by our fall from God. We all know the experience — our intellect goes off in one direction, our will in another, our emotions in yet another. This splitting of the self has produced some of the saddest divisions of modern life.

The gulf between art and science is one; the chasm between our material and spiritual power another (the more adept we become at physical survival, the less purpose or reason we seem to have for surviving at all). Cigarette smokers provide a more personal and mundane example. Countless numbers believe that smoking causes lung cancer (intellect), live in constant fear of succumbing to the dreaded disease (emotion), but still smoke (will).

It is also possible to believe in Christianity without actually being a Christian. The Bible says that demonic evil powers themselves believe in God, but this belief does not prevent them from opposing God, nor will it save them from damnation (James 2:19). Christianity says that only *faith* can heal our rift with God, not mere belief.

With the possible exception of 'sin', no Christian word has been more misunderstood than 'faith'. In the modern world Christian faith is continually confused with the inanities of secular faith. The latter is nothing but a self-willed emotional attitude: thinking positively, keeping your chin up, looking on the brighter side of life. Without any reason whatever one is supposed to hope that everything will turn out all right in the end, even though it looks bleak at the moment. This kind of faith should be called blind faith or 'faith in faith'; it has absolutely no connection with Christian faith.

Christianity is much more precise about the meaning of faith. It does not speak merely of faith, but of *faith in* God and Christ. There are several dimensions to Christian faith: intellectual, intentional (connected with the will), communal, emotional, mystical and moral. Faith encompasses the whole self. The optimism of Christian faith is not found in positive thinking, but in the power of God. In this chapter we will begin to explore Christian faith by examining its intellectual and intentional dimensions.

The test of experience

Yesterday I watched a helicopter hover overhead. What faith a helicopter pilot needs! Of course it is not blind faith. The pilot knows his machine was constructed by a reputable firm of aeronautical engineers, has a proven reliability record, is well serviced by trained mechanics and has a battery of instruments to detect any malfunction. The pilot's faith to fly the machine is based on his belief that it will operate reliably for the duration of his flight. There is only one way to test the validity of his belief — he must actually take the calculated risk of flying the helicopter.

Except perhaps for the experientially remote theorems of pure mathematics, nothing we believe or trust can ever be absolutely certain. Even the 'laws' of science are predictions founded upon degrees of probability based on past experience. Experience is the only certain test of belief. This is why no one can prove Christianity for another person. Like all belief, the most we can show about Christianity is the high probability of its truth.

But how much intellectual certainty does one need before taking the step of commitment to the Christian way? Obviously we must be sufficiently convinced to believe in the high probability of its truth. But this is a very personal matter, with moral complications. Not all of us can be expert theologians, but we will need to be convinced to the level of our own intellectual ability. Yet at root no one else is responsible for our own individual salvation or damnation. The gift of separate personality makes each of us alone, with the choice to live with or without God. In the end that choice must be made according to the light of God each has received. From peasant to professor, says Christianity, every person knows enough about God to be held responsible for the choice they make.

Morality complicates belief because the wilful immoral ego does not wish to believe in the truth of Christianity; it would rather be its own God. Although this claim could be used as a kind of blackmail into belief, it would be foolish to reject it lightly. It is not uncommon for the disbeliever to have nothing more than a childish grasp of the Christian reality map. Such failure to seek a more mature theological understanding suggests a motive other than intellectual doubts. To find God we must combine intellectual honesty with moral honesty.

Whenever an issue matters, the line between belief and doubt is always fine. For a helicopter pilot the difference between life and death depends on the reliable operation of a single motor. A pilot who flew without first checking his instruments or assuring himself that the machine was correctly serviced would be crazy. But a pilot who wanted absolute certainty would never leave the ground. Dangerous or big decisions demand careful consideration, yet we can be overcautious as well as too adventurous.

I once knew a couple who took twenty-three years to decide whether they were suitable marriage partners. By the time they finally took the marital plunge the woman had passed the age of child-bearing and they were unable to have the children they so dearly wanted. But I also know several couples who have married after knowing their partners less than six months. Nearly every one of these marriages has ended in divorce.

If religion is right, the choice about God is the most important and dangerous of all — a choice between salvation and damnation. But nowhere is the line between belief and doubt finer. God himself intends it this way. As we saw in the last chapter, unless we are free to doubt God, we are not free to love him. The coming of Christ did not alter this fundamental condition of our creation. In fact God built the possibility for doubt into the Christian solution itself.

Even a casual reading of the Gospels reveals what scholars call 'the Messianic secret'. The Gospels never depict Christ continually and blatantly claiming to be the Messiah or God. Certainly the Gospel writers claim these things about him, but he himself makes few such assertions. This has led a small number of modern secular theologians to dismiss Christ's divinity as an imaginative invention of the first Christians. But they overlook two obvious points. First that divinity, no less than human cleverness or kindness, will reveal itself in life and action, not mere claims. (As the English might say, 'A gentleman has no need to claim that he is a gentleman'.) Second that Jesus created a deliberate air of enigma about himself. According to the Gospels, he not only refused to perform miraculous proofs for doubters; he also counselled secrecy about the miracles he did perform. And Jesus deliberately used ambiguous self-designations like 'the Son of Man'. In the light of contemporary Jewish usage, this could have meant simply 'man' or it could have referred to divinity itself. Jesus left it to his hearers to decide his real meaning. With Christ, God purposefully kept the line between belief and doubt honed fine. Nothing else would maintain the freedom God intends us to have.

Saying 'yes' to God

To step from belief into faith is the only way to become a Christian. Like getting married, we can never be sure of the decision until we have made it. But unless we make it, we can never personally participate in the process which has begun to reverse the tragic consequences of humanity's fall into evil.

There are two sides to Christian faith. The first is active — something we have to do. Our spiritual personality says 'Yes' to God, not just the *yes* of language, but the *yes* of the will. There are no strict formulas to follow, but something like the following prayer will be uttered:

> *Yes God, I do want reunion with you. I want it passionately; I want to be rooted and grounded in and with you again, deeply. Amen.*

For this *yes* there is a corresponding *no*. We must say 'No' to the wilful immoral ego at the root of all human tragedy, the ego which wants to be its own God. Again there is no strict formula, but this prayer distils its essence:

> *God, I admit that I am not really God and I want to stop living as if I was. I want to start letting you be God in my life. Amen.*

Repentance and confession are the traditional Christian words to describe this active side of faith.

It is not unusual for people to come to Christian faith as the result of a personal crisis. This causes cynics to scoff, thinking such conversions prove their belief that Christian faith is a crutch for the weak. But the cynics overlook the fact that we *are* weak. Shattered relationships, illness, disillusioned hopes, death — such things catch up with us all. There is a crutch or, more fairly, a comforting side to the Christian faith.

But it is no good coming to faith with the aim of finding comfort. Comfort is to faith in Christ what good sex is to marriage — the result of a successful relationship. Sometimes it takes a personal crisis to open our eyes to the futility of a life cut off from its roots in God. Yet God is not someone we can use for our convenience. If faith aims for comfort instead of God, it will quickly be disillusioned, like the sad men who visit prostitutes in the vain hope of finding love. God is faith's true object, and faith in God takes courage — the courage to humbly own up to the selfish pride which seduces creatures to behave like creators.

In the last chapter we saw that no human effort can ever repair our broken communion with God. We might just as well expect a neuro-surgeon to excise a tumour from his own brain. Until human pride learns this lesson and admits its own spiritual bankruptcy, it will never understand the other side of Christian faith. This is the part of faith which lets the self be caught up in God's solution to the human rebellion — passively being received by God like a child being drawn by his mother's warm embrace. There is nothing we do except to allow Christ to reunite us with God. Theology has a special word to describe this process. The word is *grace*. It does not mean the prayer Christians say before meals — that is another meaning. 'Grace' means the free gift of God's love and forgiveness. A practical example will make it clearer.

There is a true story about a small Aborigine schoolboy who lived in the north of Australia. His white schoolteacher took out all her racist feelings on this black student, constantly beating and berating him. One day he reached breaking point. Tearfully he ran from the classroom and hid under the school toilet block. His teacher called the police, who used their dogs to chase him out of his hiding place like a cowering rat. Shaking with rage the teacher began to beat and berate him again, telling him he was 'a black nothing, a filthy, lazy Abo'.

But another teacher appeared in the schoolyard. Physically pushing the first teacher aside, she quietly asked the boy, 'Who are you?'

Afraid of what might happen next, and believing his answer anyway, the tiny boy replied, 'I don't know, Miss'.

The second teacher put her arms around the small black body and said, 'I know who you are. You're Harry, and I want you in my class'. That is what divine grace is like — the unexpected gift of accepting love. We cannot earn it; we can only receive it by faith.

Harry eventually grew up to become a leader of his down-trodden people. Without the accepting love of that second teacher, he almost certainly would have joined the majority of his oppressed race whose despair often leads to alcoholism and early death. The teacher's love gave him a new life and dignity.

Christianity says that, when we are received back into communion with God, we begin to participate in eternal life again. Jesus called the act of faith a *new birth*. 'You must', he said, 'be born of flesh and of the Spirit'. Without spiritual birth, we only have biological life — the birth into flesh. Unless our spirit is reborn into God's Spirit, the fading of our flesh will finally reduce it to its own tiny circle of 'aloneness' — to hell.

We can now see how misconceived is the popular picture of Christians as people trying to earn their way with God by being good. But if God restores our roots in himself by free-forgiving love, then does it matter how Christians behave? The answer is 'Yes', but goodness is the result, not the cause, of our reunion with God. The reasons behind this bald answer will emerge as we continue to explore the various dimensions of Christian faith.

Life after birth

The faith which takes the self through Christ into God is only a beginning, a birth. When we take this step, the shrivelled tendrils between our spirit and God begin to grow again. This is where the third person of God's tri-unity comes in. The Holy Spirit actually enters our own spiritual personality.

Of all experiences, this one most confirms the reality of the step from mere belief to faith. Language can hardly express it. It is as though our spirit has at last begun to ingest energy from its own reality source, just as the body needs to be constantly renewed by ingesting food from the 'out there' world of matter. But it is much more personal.

Christians try to put the experience in words by saying things like 'Now I know that God is real' or 'I feel overwhelmed by God's love'. It is an ecstatic fusing experience, like sexual love. Perhaps that is why the Bible makes marriage its chief symbol of the Christian's relationship with God. Through the Holy Spirit, God comes to us and we receive God to ourselves. The failure to satisfy the self's longing for reunion with God probably lies behind the insatiable modern pre-occupation with sex, as we shall see later.

Through the union of sperm and ovum God creates new biological life, through the relationship of persons God creates new psychic life, but through this union of spirit to Spirit God creates the highest of all life-forms — spiritual life. This is symbolically expressed by the Christian rite of baptism or christening. The old 'God-dead' self goes down under the water to die; the new 'God-alive' self comes up out of the water to new life. (For the sake of convenience, some churches only sprinkle or pour water on the candidate, but full immersion was the usual practice in New Testament times.)

There is no intention here of entering that long-standing debate about who should be baptized: whether Christ intended it only for adults with a personal faith or for the children of Christian parents too. Whatever the case, all Christians agree that the reality of baptism into the Holy Spirit is far more important than its symbolic expression as baptism in water.

Birth into the Holy Spirit begins the Christian's pilgrimage. Christ did not promise that the spiritual journey would be easy. Quite the contrary, he likened it to taking up one's cross — with all the connotations of suffering this had in the world of the Roman Empire. While they remain in this twisted and fractured world, Christians can expect spiritual pain to be added to whatever load of normal human suffering they may have to endure. But they will find that their suffering is now imbued with the meaning of Christ's own suffering — not futile torture of the self ending in nothingness, but labour pains leading to full restoration with God.

Spiritual suffering derives from the tension generated as the Holy Spirit seeks to transform us into the perfected humanity of Christ, the new Adam. No Christian will ever reach that ideal in this life. But each Christian will, like Christ, be locked into a continual battle with evil, both inner and outer. The Christian will always be the critic, judging both self and world against a standard external to both. Sometimes this will draw the hatred of self-interested defenders of the status quo. Yet neither exile, imprisonment or nailing to a cross can destroy the freedom which answers to none but God.

God knows how much suffering each one of us can bear, promising (in the words of the Apostle Paul) that no one will be tested beyond what God knows we can endure. Hence it is false to doubt God because of another's suffering; God knows what it is like to be in that person's skin, but we do not.

On our own journey we will always encounter new selfishness and pride, even surgings of renewed doubt. At times we will stumble and fall, and there will be some sins we never seem able to escape. Like the last stages of a marathon foot race, the nearer we seem to be approaching the finishing line of Christ-like perfection, the harder it becomes to make any progress at all.

Those who have got near tell of an experience they call 'the dark night of the soul', when suddenly life turns ashen and empty — as if, like Christ's experience on the cross, God has totally forsaken them. There will be moments in every Christian's life when something like this happens, times when they do not even know how to form a prayer seeking help. But then they will discover the Holy Spirit's great paradox, the paradox of joy in the midst of suffering. The very Spirit who has pushed them to the brink will now begin weeping inwardly with them. As St Paul says:

> *The Spirit comes to aid our weakness. We do not even know how we ought to pray, but through our inarticulate groans the Spirit himself pleads for us, and God who searches our inmost being knows what the Spirit means'* (Romans 8:26-27).

Paradoxically these words describe an experience language cannot adequately capture — of being understood even when we do not understand ourselves. But that is how joy can co-exist with suffering. We see the two sides of this process in the faces of great Christians some call 'saints'. Though lined with the scars of huge suffering, their faces seem aglow with inner tranquility and strength. They bear living witness to St Paul's view that Christian suffering is like an athletic contest, each new trial increasing the strength and endurance of the spirit.

Deliberate emphasis has been given to the suffering side of the Christian pilrimage because often it gets left out altogether. Many people begin the Christian journey, only to find disillusionment when the jubbly-bubbly happiness they were falsely promised fails to last. Happiness is a fleeting emotion occasioned by passing circumstances. Falling in love, a good night out, even drugs can produce happiness but not joy. Joy is the characteristic emotion of the Christian faith, the emotion generated inside us by the Holy Spirit. Joy comes from being grounded in the eternal being of God. The flux of circumstances can vary joy, but never destroy it. Joy turns the water of ordinary happiness into wine, and the bitter draught of suffering into medicine.

A problem that easily becomes an excuse

But what happens to all those people who have not found reunion with God by faith in Christ, especially those who have never even heard of him? What about all the sincere followers of non-Christian religions? Are they on the road to damnation? And what about those who have never really rejected Christ, but have been turned off Christianity by some unfortunate experience with the church or a minister — what happens to them?

Strictly speaking no Christian can venture to give

complete answers to these questions, because God has not revealed them. But some answers can be given with certainty and others tentatively inferred. First, after death every person who has received God's free-forgiving love — by putting their faith in Christ — will enter God's full presence with all their sin and suffering evaporated to nothing. Second, no one can be reunited with God except through Christ's reversal of the fall into evil. Third, there is only one free, created being for whose life God will hold us ultimately responsible, our own self. Until we have sorted out our own standing with God, we are probably just making excuses by worrying about the standing of others. Fourth, the Bible itself clearly teaches that reunion with God through Christ is possible even for those who have never heard of Christ. This is hardly surprising, for otherwise every human being who lived before the birth of Christ would be damned without a chance, including all the Old Testament saints.

From these answers, and what has already been said about damnation in an earlier chapter, we can safely infer that God will judge each one of us according to our response to whatever light we have received from him. Paul says that Abraham was put right with God by faith in God as he knew him (Romans 4:22). To summarize: no one will be damned except those who choose to be damned, and no one will be restored except through Christ's reversal of the fall into evil.

* * *

God's grace, his free-forgiving love, became possible by what he did in and through Jesus Christ.

Christ brought a greater revolution to religion than Newton and Einstein brought to science, or Marx brought to politics. In terms of our earlier analogy between religion and archery, divine grace received through faith in Christ scores the bull's-eye.

Divine grace is the fundamental difference between Judaism and Islam on the one hand and Christianity on the other. Both Judaism and Islam are full of ideas about free-forgiving love — as might be expected with religions which claim to follow the same God as Christianity — but, without Christ, they are unable to reconcile divine love and forgiveness with human evil and the need for just punishment. Both religions tend to fall back on the futile attempt to earn one's way with God by being good. And without any sense of God's own suffering for humanity, neither Judaism nor Islam can fully picture the depth of the divine compassion for suffering human beings which Christ revealed.

When Jesus was born in ancient Israel, his fellow Jews dared not even pronounce the basic Hebrew name for God. They wrote it JHWH, and to this day nobody really knows what vowels should be pronounced between these four consonants (vowels were usually inferred, not written in ancient Hebrew). But through God's love revealed in Christ, the first Christians, all of whom were Jews, began praying to God as *Abba* — the most intimate form of the Semitic word meaning 'Father'. Grace produced a revolution in their relationship with God which even filtered down to the name by which they addressed him.

In Islam God certainly loves. But though metaphysically Muslims regard Allah as being as close to them as their jugular veins, in terms of personal relationship he appears distant, overbearing and somewhat fierce. Submission to the inexorable divine will seems to characterize a Muslim's sense of relationship with God, not the 'communion in separateness' of reciprocated love between creature and Creator. Nowhere does Islam reach the depths of the divine love that was nailed to Calvary's cross.

Hopefully no Christian would be so foolish as to claim that Christians behave better than Jews or Muslims, but in theory they should. For only the knowledge of a God who suffered at the hands of his enemies can give weight to Christ's command, 'Love your enemies and do good to those that hate you'.

19

We become our relationships

CHRISTIAN COMMUNITY

As people in secular countries turn their backs on God, identity crises become more common. With no sense of journeying anywhere, many people suffer breakdowns. Thousands escape into alcoholism or drugs. Millions try to avoid the yawning chasm within the self by living out the pretend phantasies we explored in the chapter on secularism. But it is also becoming popular to search, as people say, for one's 'true self' or 'real identity', as if this mysterious entity is hidden somewhere inside us all.

If it were possible to peel off every layer of our self, it would be like peeling an onion. At the end there would be nothing — no core at all, just a potential for becoming. We uncovered this fact with the example of the monkey boy in *Part One*. Without human relationships, the self remains an empty potential. But as it develops by learning a language and conversing with other selves, so the self also acquires an identity as the member of a family, a culture and a part of human history. Until we reach the age of self-conscious reflection, this identity seems as inalterable and given as the laws of nature itself. We *are* our relationships.

There is no 'real self' or 'true identity' hiding inside us; identity is a matter of relationships. But when we acquire the ability for self-conscious reflection, we can change our identity by changing our relationships. For example I can choose to reject my cultural identity as an Australian in favour of a Greek identity, but I only become Greek if I go and live among Greeks in Greece or in one of their ethnic communities here in Australia. Conversely Greeks, trying to maintain their cultural identity in Australia or the United States, will need to maintain a close circle of relationships with fellow Greeks or their identity will be swallowed up by the majority culture. No one can easily maintain an identity others fail to confirm. It may be a fact that I am the world's greatest soprano, but I shall not be able to maintain this belief for long if it is only confirmed by my bathroom walls. We *become* the relationships we choose. If we wish to maintain a particular identity, we need to choose our relationships carefully.

A universal community

According to Christianity ultimately nothing is real in itself except God. If we want a 'real self' or 'true identity', we can only find it in a relationship with God. It is the entry of the Holy Spirit which gives the self a core. But God does not just relate to us as individuals in the abstract. Now that we have seen how God makes us bodily and physically 'in' and 'through' other human beings, it should not surprise us that this is how he makes us spiritually too.

All identity is formed in the crucible of interpersonal relationships; this is the fundamental fact of human personality. A lone Marxist in a Christian community will find it hard to maintain identity as a Marxist, and vice versa. Even atheists, flat-earthers and astrologers form themselves into clubs to help maintain their identity. Because of their relationship with God, lone Christians have successfully maintained their faith, even in such hostile circumstances as the solitary confinement of a Nazi prison cell. But without the historical community which received and transmitted the faith down the centuries, there would be no Christians at all, lone or otherwise.

Only simplistic or short-sighted people remain unaware of the terrible shortcomings of their own community. The vast majority of Christians are not naive. They know more about the sins of the Church than any Marxist or atheist critic. Christians live with the Church's sins; Marxists and atheists do not. In fact most Christians will not only admit the evils of the Church; they will confess to adding to them too. The last chapter made it clear that Christians are not perfect people, but forgiven sinners trying to let the Holy Spirit make them more like Jesus Christ. They realize that some Church members, perhaps even a few of its leaders, are not sincere, but merely use the Church for personal power, status, even financial gain. But because the Church is a community of the forgiven, not the perfect, it is hard to tell who are sheep and who are wolves in sheep's clothing. Sometimes the Church is forced to make a judgment and expel a member, but this is done with fear and trembling because only God knows what is going on inside a person.

Christians do not believe the Church is just a human invention, but a mystical or historical extension of God's own being. The Church would have fulfilled the ever repeated prophecies of its opponents and perished long ago if it was just a human institution. Christians choose to belong to the Church with all its warts and cancers because, through it, God provides the nutriment for spiritual growth. Refusing to belong to the Church because its members are imperfect is like refusing food in a restaurant because the chef has a temper and the waiter a mistress.

Christ himself founded the Church. He said that when the Holy Spirit channeled God's presence to us it would come to 'ye' the plural, not just 'thou' the singular. (This is clear in the original Greek of the New Testament which distinguishes between *you* singular and plural, like Old English.) This explains Jesus' saying that, 'Whenever two or three are gathered together in my name, there am I in the midst'. Sometimes this is crudely interpreted to mean that Christ is present in church, invisibly sitting on an altar or in a vacant pew. But the Church is the community of faith, not a building. What Jesus meant is that when Christians meet together, God is especially present in and through each to the other: a personal presence through persons.

God gave Paul the Apostle the task of implementing Jesus' teaching about the Christian community. Paul taught that spiritual birth is both a birth into the Holy Spirit and into the body of Christ (his cryptic name for the Church). The example of the monkey boy demonstrated that, unless we are born into a human community as well as the world of nature, we cannot reach the full potential of our being. It is similar with spiritual life. It is not enough to simply experience a personal rebirth; to fully realize our spiritual potential we need to belong to a Christian community. St Paul said that just as the biological body is made up of many interrelated parts (cells, lungs, arms, legs and so on), each Christian forms a vital interdependent part of Christ's body, the Church. And just as each part of the biological body is nerve-linked to the brain, each Christian's spirit is mystically and spiritually fused to Christ as the head of the Church (see Ephesians 1:23 and 1 Corinthians 12:12-26).

We can think of the Church as a continuation of the divine presence, poured into the human flesh and personality of Jesus Christ. In Jesus that presence remained clear and unsullied; in ordinary Christians it will be twisted and bent. Yet God mercifully preserves his presence by continually reforming the Church, even causing revolutionary upheavals to recall the Church to the precepts of its ever-present Founder. Failure to let God make our self part of the Christian community will stifle our spiritual potential, much like inability to share human community stifled the monkey boy's mental and psychic potential. Spiritual life is formed and nurtured in the spiritual community, just as personal life is formed and nurtured in the community of persons.

God gave the Church for our spiritual nourishment. Christians do all sorts of activities in the community of the Church. They study the Bible together, discuss and share problems of believing and living, hear sermons and lectures by theologians, weep with each other in sorrow and laugh with each other in joy. But at the centre of it all is worship.

Mature dependence

Psychology and psychotherapy are only now beginning to escape Freud's terrible mistake about human maturity and functioning, a mistake which has become part and parcel of the popular thinking of secularists. Freud equated mature human functioning with personal independence and tight rational control of one's self and life experiences. Consequently the Freudian picture of adult maturity left no room for child-like regression to dependence upon anyone. All dependence was childish. As the essence of worship is child-like dependence upon God, worship could have no place in Freud's image of mature adult life. This lies behind the popular secularist tendency to view church-going as a prop for the weak.

Because he put rational consciousness above all other forms of consciousness, Freud assigned art a similar fate to religion. Like religion, art deals in worlds of consciousness that are mythic, symbolic and ritualist. But however fine its achievements in music, poetry or painting, at root Freud considered all art to be the product of neurotic, immature sexuality. Not even his recurrent fainting spells could persuade Freud to modify this equation of maturity and tight rational control of one's self and world.

Today among the practitioners of Freud's craft, there is growing recognition that maturity entails the ability to make appropriate shifts between dependent and independent modes of consciousness. A man who day-dreams at work about being in his wife's arms when writing a computer program has entered an inappropriate, symbolic, dependent mode of consciousness. He should be concentrating on his job. His wife will judge the reverse situation as being equally inappropriate.

In everyday life the world of things and work is generally the appropriate time for the consciousness of tight rational control. For some jobs (e.g. a steeplejack) one's life depends upon maintaining it. But this mode of consciousness drains our energy and mechanizes our personal life. This is partly why people rush from their factories and offices at the end of the day. On the way home they begin to make the transition to more dependent modes of consciousness: reading the paper in the bus, dropping in to the pub for a drink with friends, listening to the car radio as they drive. At home they more fully enter symbolic dependent modes of consciousness: relaxing in a favourite armchair, sleeping and dreaming, engaging in casual conversation with friends, making love. These are the person-renewing modes of consciousness.

Mature human functioning is now seen as the ability to enter the appropriate mode of consciousness at the appropriate time. Fixation on one or other of the poles of consciousness may be defined as immature functioning. A workaholic is fixated at the rational, independent mode and an alcoholic at the symbolic, dependent mode.

We saw earlier that God made human beings to find their fulfilment in a life of communion in separateness with him. For Christianity, worship is the tap-root of divine communion. Worship is to the human spirit what water is to the human body; it is the spirit-renewing mode of consciousness. From the primal origins of human consciousness recollected in the Old Testament has come the divine command to worship in community once each seven days. Hopefully contemporary views about psychic maturity will result in secularists and Marxists rethinking their need to worship God. What is worship? We can think of worship like this.

Imagine a mother taking her little boy to the seaside for the first time. The child is both fascinated and frightened by the waves breaking at the water's edge. He stays clinging to his mother, distantly watching the waves. Gradually he works up the courage to take a few steps in the water's direction, but quickly returns to cling to his mother once more. Again and again this process is repeated, each time the boy getting a little closer to the edge. Even after he finally succeeds and has spent many hours playing in the water, the child periodically returns to his mother. Clinging renews his courage and security in this new, seaside world. His mother's arms give deeply emotional and symbolic assurance that this world is all right. From finding treasures like discarded cigarette butts to learning how to relate safely to waves, the child's explorations mark the beginning of rational enquiry and control.

Worship is dependently clinging to God: the transcendent self returning from its wanderings in the mysterious world of things and mortals to find renewal in the Eternal Source. If human beings are like children before the immensity of the material universe, how much more they are like children before the Being who invented the material universe! Worship is not childish but child-like trust in God's love and protection.

What words cannot say

A lot of reality cannot be captured in language or surface realism, especially personal reality. Portraits can 'say' things about people which photographs can never depict. Fine music can distil emotions that are inexpressible in words. The words 'I love you and will protect you' could not tell the child at the seaside what his mother's physical touch told him.

Christians deliberately create a world of ritual and symbol to help transform consciousness into the spirit-renewing mode of worship. Some Christians do this elaborately, with sublime architecture, music, liturgies and art; others believe it should be done well, but simply. Unless the grander rituals and symbols become idolatrous objects of worship themselves, in which case they should be eliminated, the style of worship is probably just a matter of individual taste.

But all Christians value one symbolic ritual above all others, because Christ himself commanded them to use it. Some denominations call it the Lord's Supper; others the Eucharist, the Mass or Holy

Communion. Some think it is so important that it should be celebrated every week; others think it is so important it should only be celebrated once or twice a year, lest repetition dull its meaning. But whatever its name or frequency, Christians agree that it is the outward and visible symbol of the deepest inward and spiritual reality of their faith.

Even everyday rituals and symbols appear foolish to anyone not participating in their inner meaning. Personally I am a great admirer of the ideals of American democracy. Yet all the ritual symbolic razzle-dazzle of the party political conventions looks quite ridiculous to me. But I know in my head that this expression of grass-roots enthusiasm is somehow vital for maintaining democratic freedom. Without a relationship with God, Holy Communion (its name in my denomination) probably looks silly to outsiders too. A group of otherwise sensible adults gathering around a table to eat bits of bread and take sips of wine — what is all this about?

Christ said the bread and wine represent his body and blood given in sacrifice for human sin on the cross. When Christians eat the bread and drink the wine — with faith in Christ's spiritual presence — they renew the communion with God made possible by that sacrifice. But words cannot express the depth of meaning in this symbol. And if symbols can 'say' what language cannot say, then we must not expect language to have the ability to explain how symbols work. If Christians had followed this principle, they might have avoided much futile argumentation about how Holy Communion works. Yet they all agree that it does work. Somehow eating the bread and drinking the wine brings a sense of great closeness to God.

I once witnessed a moving example of how Holy Communion can convey what language fails to convey. (This is not to downgrade language: Bible readings, sermons and verbal prayers are all essential parts of Christian worship too.) I had been worshipping in a church where each Sunday for many years a husband and wife always sat in a front pew with their mentally retarded, teenage son. The boy was perfectly behaved, but usually looked passive, sad and bored. When his parents went to receive the sacrament, he always remained behind in the pew. One day the clergyman took his parents aside after church and suggested the boy be allowed to receive communion himself. At first they resisted, saying their son's mental condition would prevent him understanding its meaning. But the clergyman eventually persuaded them to give it a try. So after some simple explanation about what he was to do, the next Sunday the boy knelt with his parents to receive the bread and wine. The light and smile on his face testified to the clergyman's wise counsel. We know that although the mentally retarded may be incapable of deep rational conversation, they can give and respond to physical affection. This experience showed that without much ability to understand sermons or the Bible, they can still respond to God's embrace too.

Immature worship

But worship can fail. It fails when we do not find renewal in child-like return to our spirit's source. This happens for two opposite reasons. First, there are some people who fail to let go the tight rational self of their secular workaday world. They want church worship to bristle with rational meaning, and so the rituals and symbols never work — like trying to read poetry with all head and no heart. They complain that the service is the same every week and that repetition destroys its meaning. But they are really seeking spiritual entertainment, not God.

I am writing this book in the totally familiar surroundings of my own study. I know that if I tried to write in a less familiar location, say the university library, I would be continually distracted, especially by all the attractive female students walking past my desk there. Similarly a church service is meant to be familiar, familiar enough to lift our consciousness to God and not to draw attention to itself. A person who will not let the self journey in periodic return to its spiritual womb will soon give up going to church altogether, complaining of its irrationality and meaninglessness.

Second, there are people who perpetually remain in worship's passive, dependent mode of consciousness. They live in a pious dream-world and are often called religious fanatics. They mistake their dependence upon the Church for dependence upon God. Neglecting their families, their work and their duties as responsible citizens of the state, they try to spend every spare moment in religious activities. They become churchaholics. Through the Holy Spirit, God is always as near to us as our own breath, but we are not meant to remain fixed in the heightened awareness that worship gives to his presence. To expect to live the Christian life continually soaring through the ecstasy of worship consciousness is as distorted as seeking to live a married life on the peaks of orgasm consciousness. Communion *in* separateness is the Christian ideal, not separateness without communion or communion without separateness.

Worship fails most when it tries to use God for comfort or renewal, but does not transform the moral life of the worshipper. Failure in worship is the real origin of Marx's complaint that God is an invention to justify the wealth of the rich and a pious phantasy to soothe the worldly sufferings of the poor. But true worship will not only renew the sources of personal life by regressing in dependence upon God; it will also invest the worshipper with the qualities of God's own character. To worship God on Sunday and live like a selfish pagan for the rest of the week is not to worship God at all. Eight centuries before Christ and twenty-seven before Marx, the prophet Amos thundered these words in the divine name:

> *You that turn justice upside down . . .*
> *levy taxes on the poor and extract a tribute of grain from them . . .*
> *who persecute the guiltless . . .*
> *and thrust the destitute out of court . . .*
> *I hate, I spurn your pilgrim feasts; I will not delight in the noise of your sacred ceremonies* (Amos 5:7, 11-12 and 21).

When worship produces pious rituals without ethical transformation and social justice, it is opium to God as well as Karl Marx!

We become our relationship with God. When God

took human suffering upon himself through the sufferings of Christ, a new vision of God was revealed — and a new vision of suffering humanity too. Christ explicitly taught that all human suffering was his suffering, like a child's suffering is his/her parents' suffering. We can never fully know what other people suffer, even our own children, because they are inside their suffering and we are outside. Only God knows a person's suffering from the inside. Christ said that whenever we see suffering in another person, we see the suffering of God in Christ again. Whether it be the poor, the sick, the imprisoned or the lonely, Christ said that God will judge our response to human suffering as our response to him (Matthew 25:31-46). Justice and compassion are the tests of whether we are worshipping God or an idol.

Because we do become our relationships, neglect of the communal dimensions of faith will retard spiritual growth. We do not need guilt feelings to bribe us to consume food, nor do we need them to induce church membership and worship. Anyone sincerely seeking the life of 'communion in separateness' with God will be driven to church membership and worship by spiritual hunger pains. But there is also a private life-flow between us and God — prayer. Some people believe science has made nonsense of prayer; others only pray when they get into trouble, calling upon God like some kind of divine ambulance man. In the next chapter we will try to make sense of this mystical and spiritual dimension of faith.

20 Ultimate intimacy

PRAYER

Some years ago my father discovered a large tumour in his throat. The doctor did not know whether it was malignant or benign, but it needed urgent surgical removal. I was terribly upset. What was I to pray? My thoughts turned in every direction.

'God knows everything, so God does not need me to inform him about the tumour. Yet what if the tumour is cancerous? Should I ask God to manipulate its cellular structure and cure my father? Can God do that sort of thing anyway? And even if he can, does God take any notice of prayers like that? Besides my father is getting old. Some day God is going to let him die — perhaps this tumour will do it. I cannot always expect a cure, so why now?'

Petitionary prayer — the prayer that asks God to do things — is probably the most difficult, but not the most important kind of prayer. We shall explore it first.

Petitionary prayer

Obviously God can interfere in the regular workings of the universe if he wants to. The workings are only regular because he makes them that way. But when does God want to interfere? Plainly not very often — and we should be glad. Human beings could not survive long in a random universe. Imagine the chaos if from time to time without warning half the cars on freeways suddenly slipped into reverse gear. Imagine the destruction if gravity occasionally reversed or the earth missed a couple of rotations. Think of the hangovers if all water periodically turned into wine. If God answered every prayer with a miracle, either this universe would become dangerously random or he would have to create an entirely different universe. The present universe is bent and twisted, but it is not random. A random universe would be hell on earth.

God's relationship to our universe is like an author's to his novel. The author creates the novel but is outside the book's stream of events; he is not even in the same time sequence. Between the villain firing the shot and the heroine falling down dead, the author can eat lunch or take a nap. Yet there is a difference. The characters in God's 'novel' have a life of their own, because God has given them a certain amount of freedom to write their own plots. According to Christianity, God does take account of our requests and listens with love and sympathy to our petitionary prayers. But he never interferes in a way that would destroy our freedom or render the universe random.

No one except God knows the result of events before they even happen and no one else has the power to bring good from evil. Thus God often answers prayer by giving us what is best, not necessarily what we want. Christ died the death of the damned not because he wanted it, but because it was best. Christ also performed miracles as signs of God's power and intention to ultimately restore this twisted universe. Sometimes for reasons no one can explain, God still performs such miracles in response to prayer. Perhaps they are also meant as signs. But we cannot expect all the dead to be raised, all the sick healed, all destructive storms stilled or enough good wine for all to celebrate — at least not until God makes the universe anew.

Before I say what prayer I offered for my father, or what happened to him, let us complicate the problem of petitionary prayer a little more. Suppose a group of Christians is planning a weekend retreat to the country. Because they hope to spend lots of time outdoors, they pray for fine weather. But all around the sleepy township where they intend to stay are vineyards withering from drought. That very week many of the local farmers gather in the local church to pray for rain to save their dying crops. Doesn't this make nonsense of petitionary prayer? And is not nonsense compounded when it rains the whole weekend and the farmers thank God for saving their crops and the visitors thank him for bringing them all closer together by keeping them inside — or, if it does not rain, the visitors thank God for sunshine and the farmers explain it as a test of their faith?

Today we have electronic computers which can sort thousands of data inputs in a fraction of a second. God is not limited by time at all, but computers have made it much easier for mere mortals to imagine how God can hear and respond to millions of prayers at once. He could easily take account of a million conflicting requests about weather from all over the earth. But presumably God does not usually interfere with weather patterns at all. The Gospels make it quite obvious that when Jesus stilled a storm on Lake Galilee, the exceptional nature of the act allowed it to be a sign of the restoration God was preparing. Though still in its infancy, weather forecasting relies on penetrating through to the rational pattern behind all atmospheric behaviour. Satellites have recently taken this science a great leap forward. We can no longer think that because particular natural events are mysterious to us they are not ordered according to regular, rational laws. Indeed the rational structure of the universe, though bent and twisted with evil, still testifies to its source in the rational mind of God. Which is not to say that God cannot perform miracles with weather or change the malign cells of a throat tumour to benign cells. But miracle is not God's normal way of dealing with us and our world. It is not wrong but it is foolish to pray prayers which take little account of God's *normal* dealing with the world.

What I prayed for my father was this:

> *Lord, you already know that my father has a tumour and you already know that I don't want him to die. I know that some day he will die and that I will have to cope without his friendship, but does it have to be so soon? You know his fears and that he feels he still has lots of things to live for here. Let him know that he is in your hands whatever happens. If he has to die soon, let us both feel your love even if we cannot presently understand your design. Amen.*

Perhaps some Christians would say this prayer lacks the faith to produce a miracle. But prayer is not magic. God cannot be manipulated by faith or anything else. My father's tumour was benign. I have no way of telling whether God worked a miracle or not, but we all thanked him for the result. A few weeks ago my father had a heart attack; we found no reason for changing the form of prayer we had used with the tumour.

A deeper view of prayer

Jesus' first disciples were confused about prayer so they asked him to teach them how to pray. This is what Jesus taught:

> *When you pray, do not be like the hypocrites! They love to stand up and pray in the synagogues and on the street corners so that everybody will see them. Remember this! They have already been paid in full. But when you pray, go to your room and close the door, and pray to your Father who is unseen. And your Father, who sees what you do in private, will reward you.*
>
> *In your prayers do not use a lot of words, as the pagans do, who think that God will hear them because of their long prayers. Do not be like them; your Father already knows what you need before you ask him. This is the way you should pray:*
>
> *Our Father in heaven:*
> *May your name be kept holy,*
> *May your Kingdom come,*
> *May your will be done on earth as it is in heaven.*

Give us today the food we need;
Forgive us the wrongs that we have done,
As we forgive the wrongs that others have done us;
Do not bring us to hard testing, but keep us safe from the Evil One (Matthew 6:5-15).

It would take a chapter to traverse the artfully simple depths of Jesus' meaning, but clearly its centre is the secret inner life with God. We are so accustomed to relating to other persons through language that some people think prayer is folly because God does not talk back audibly. Yet again and again our journey has brought us up against the limitations of language communication. Language is the vehicle we use to project our inner person across to other inner persons. Language lifts us up out of the world of nature and into the world of transcendent consciousness, but it leaves us stranded too. It works reasonably well in ordinary circumstances, but is almost hopeless for conveying the deepest recesses of personal life — our profoundest loves, despair, grief or joy.

Through prayer we establish a relationship no language or art can reach, a relationship of inner person to inner person direct. We use words but silence, images, groans, cries and soundless singing too. As Jesus said, there is no need to babble on or to recite things God already knows. But there is a discipline of prayer, the discipline of setting aside time and place to enter a relationship more intimate than telling one's secrets to a friend or making love with one's spouse.

God certainly 'talks back', but not through the ear

drum because he is not 'out there' in time and space. In prayer we hear the voice of God in language, images, intuitions, reverie, rhythms, inward glows, silence — everything the inner self is capable of experiencing. But there is a danger. Through sin we can all too easily twist our own thoughts and feelings into the voice of God. That is why we need the Christian reality map and the Christian community, so that we can test objectively what we have heard subjectively in private.

The dark side of prayer

Not long ago the little daughter of a prominent English clergyman was in hospital ill with leukemia. Each day her father came to visit. There was a church near the hospital and on his way the clergyman always stopped there to pray. One day it was the little girl's birthday, so her father bought a cake with candles. As always, he stopped on the way to pray inside the church. When he reached the hospital, he found his daughter had died. Quickly leaving, he went back to the church and hurled the cake at the crucifix standing on the altar, knocking it down.

Some people pray as if God is a frail old maiden aunt. They seem to think God cannot take our dark side — our grief, despair and anger. But they kid themselves, not God. God knows our dark side without being told. It is we who need to pour our dark side out to God for healing. Nothing destroys a relationship with God more than simmering inside with anger against him, except perhaps trying to pretend that we do not even have such feelings. Was the English clergyman's cake-hurling a defiant act of impious sacrilege, or was he still within the circle of a passionate relationship with God?

Those who believe spiritual propriety dictates they expose only their 'light' side to God need to be prescribed heavy doses of meditation upon the Old Testament Psalms and the Book of Job. Job lost all his children. He lost his fortune too. But what finally broke him was a painful skin disease, interminably itchy, producing running sores from head to foot. Job let go with a prayer that came very close to cursing God himself:

> *Perish the day when I was born and the night which said, 'A man-child is conceived!'*
> *May that day turn to darkness; may God above not look for it . . .*
> *May it wait for a dawn that never comes;*
> *nor ever see the eyelids of the morning,*
> *because it did not shut the doors of the womb that bore me* (Job 3:3-4 and 9-10).

Job's friends try to chide and comfort him with theological answers full of reason's light, but they are all too slick for Job's dark sufferings. At the end of the book it is they, not Job, whom God chides for misbehaviour. Job is only able to come full circle and return to God by keeping the full range of his inner life open and exposed. By taking his anger and despair into the divine relationship, Job discovered a spiritual certainty only great wrestlers with God can find. This is Job's prayer at the end:

> *I know that thou canst do all things*
> *and that no purpose is beyond thee.*
> *But I have spoken of great things*
> *which I have not understood,*

things too wonderful for me to know.
I knew of thee then only by report,
but now I see thee with mine own eyes.
Therefore I melt away;
I repent in dust and ashes (Job 42:2-6).

'Wrestle' is the word that best describes the Christian's inner life with God. For there is a sense in which God forces us to wrench the meaning and joy of life out of him. This may shock some pietists, but it is there in the Bible itself. Secularists will not want to hear of it, because they like their meanings cheap and their thrills easy. Jesus' temptation in the wilderness is an example too profound to explore in the brief space of this chapter. But an incident in the life of Jacob the Old Testament patriarch will serve nearly as well.

Jacob's basic problem was as simple as any of us might face. He is returning home after years of living away. A messenger comes to inform him that Esau, the brother he once betrayed, is coming to meet him on the way. Jacob is drenched with fear. Is Esau coming to kill him in revenge? Why then had God commanded him to return home? We are not told explicitly, but presumably Jacob's guilt about the old betrayal is streaming up from his unconscious self. Hoping to placate his elder brother's supposed wrath, he sends presents ahead for him. By now it is nightfall and this is how the Bible tells the story:

And Jacob was left alone; and a man wrestled with him until the breaking of the day. When the man saw that he did not prevail against Jacob, he touched the hollow of his thigh; and Jacob's thigh was put out of joint as he wrestled with him. Then he said, 'Let me go, for the day is breaking'.

But Jacob said; 'I will not let you go, unless you bless me'.

And he said to him, 'What is your name?'

And he said 'Jacob'.

Then he said, 'Your name shall no more be called Jacob, but Israel (meaning God strove*), for you have striven with God and with men, and have prevailed'.*

Then Jacob asked him, 'Tell me, I pray, your name'.

But he said, 'Why is it that you ask my name?' And there he blessed him. So Jacob called the name of that place Penuel (meaning Face of God*), saying, 'For I have seen God face to face, and yet my life is preserved'. The sun rose upon him as he passed Penuel, limping because of his thigh* (Genesis 32:24-32).

Guilt and fear will not let Jacob drift into sleep's oblivion or renewing dreams. This ancient insomnia is not at all unlike the sleepless tossing in a million beds last night. But instead of drowning the fretful self in drug or alcoholic stupor, there is a wrestle. At first a merely human wrestle. With himself? With a mythic, internal Esau? Perhaps both. But then the wrestle sinks deeper, into a wrestle with God and yet somehow still with men too. God is pressed for a blessing. Maybe the blessing of forgiveness. Maybe the blessing of courage or hope. Maybe the blessing of assurance that it is right to return home. Probably the lot.

And all this between the stark existences of dusk and dawn, earth and sky. God presses Jacob and injures him in the region of the groin, that place which aches dully with pleasure after the spasms of sexual orgasm. With dangerous pride at his own strength, Jacob demands to know God's name. To 'name' is to control: careful classification of data is the first step of scientific discovery. God answers Jacob with a question to which silence is the only reply, and then God blesses him. Now Jacob is such another person, his self is renamed. As day breaks he goes on his way, injured but healed.

This episode is a pattern of the Christian's inner life with God, the sun always rising on us as we go limping on our way.

Now, at last, we can go to where many will think we should have been first — to the sources and conditions of the Christian moral life.

21
About fruit trees and love

FACE-TO-FACE CHRISTIAN MORALITY

This book began with a tragic picture of human personality, a picture of sentient beings trapped on a dumb treadmill of matter and time, trying to eke out a little happiness before it wears them down to oblivion. But we rejected that picture as incapable of explaining all the facts. We saw that personality is not a tragic accident, but a doorway into an eternal reality which is itself personal. But tragedy remained — not the tragedy of personal life trapped in an immense impersonal universe, but the tragedy of sin. This is sin as cause not symptom — a person willing his/her own self to be God. Then we saw what God did to reverse our fatal abuse of freedom and what we must do to participate in God's solution.

We cannot make sense of Christian morality until we understand the place of the personal on the Christian reality map. Otherwise Christian morality, which is meant to rescue the personality from impersonality, becomes a set of grey, repressive rules turning people into things. Until we see that personality is spiritual, we cannot account for the elemental world of good and evil in which it lives, moves and has its being. On the scale of nature, animal life is closest to our own. Yet no animal has ever devised the subtle cruelties human beings commonly wreak on each other. There is no animal equivalent of Adolph Hitler or Joseph Stalin. Spiritual beings do not wrestle merely with flesh and blood, but with the demonic powers of darkness unleashed by sin. From sin itself comes 'sins'. Those who will the self *against* God also will their self *as* God over others. Most of us do not have the opportunity to will our self as God over Germany or Russia, but we do have our marriages, our children and those below us on the social pecking order.

This chapter will explore the sources and conditions of Christian morality in the context of face-to-face relationships. The final chapter will apply these sources and conditions to the complex webs of social structural relationships. In this chapter we will see why God's free forgiveness of sin and sins is not a recipe for immorality, but for the highest morality of all. We will try to understand why Christians are always going on about sexual morality. And we will attempt to explain why, if some atheists behave better than most Christians, this does not undermine the essential truth of Christianity.

We project what is in us

Christian theology insists that morality is not a 'chicken and egg' problem. Goodness does not produce our relationship with God; it is the other way around. Our relationship with God produces goodness. Moral behaviour is an external projection of what we are like inside, in our spirit. A television set with a cracked transistor projects a distorted picture, however clear the signal it receives. Or, as Jesus said:

> *Can grapes be picked from briars, or figs from thistles? In the same way a good tree always yields good fruit, and a poor tree bad fruit* (Matthew 7:16-17).

We do what we are. The only way to remove the symptoms of evil is to cure the disease of the spirit.

God's 'free-forgiving' love is the cure — it goes to the root of the problem. But why does this love begin to change our evil projections into good? We started to see the answer in an earlier chapter. It is because of the new inner presence of God the Holy Spirit. This has little to do with rules and regulations and everything to do with our personal relationship with God. We can think of the motives for Christian morality under two headings: appropriateness and love. First, appropriateness.

Most people consider cockroaches dirty creatures. There is a television advertisement which plays on this reaction. It shows an elegant formal dinner party in a private home. Both hosts and guests are magnificently dressed. The table is set with the finest lace and silver. As coffee is served, the hostess removes the lid of an ornate sugar bowl and out jump several small cockroaches. She and her husband blush with shame. The guests gasp in horror, and a dubbed voice now informs viewers that they can avoid similar embarrassment by purchasing a new brand of powerful insect spray. It is all rather melodramatic of course, but nevertheless a clever manipulation of our sense of appropriateness and inappropriateness. If cockroaches do not give us the shivers, then we can appreciate the point by substituting another nasty, say a live rat under the meat-tray lid.

God's love carries the divine goodness directly into our own spirit by the presence of the Holy Spirit. God dwells within us. In this presence petty selfishness or unkind thoughts about others glare inappropriately like a rat under the meat-tray lid — to say nothing of bigger sins like hate, jealousy, gossip, bitterness, violence, lies and hypocrisy. Rats are all right in sewers, but not on dinner tables. We know the divine guest deserves a palace or a temple to dwell in, yet God is so full of free-forgiving love we never hear any direct word of judgment or condemnation. By just being what he is, the Holy Spirit tells us what kind of behaviour is appropriate and what is inappropriate. His presence gives us a deep desire to will sins out of our lives — to behave with appropriateness in our new relationship of 'communion in separateness' with God.

But there is something besides will and appropriateness too. Filled with God's accepting love, we feel a new power in our own wills: love power.

Love: a word worth rehabilitating

After 'God' no word matters more to Christianity than *love*. The Bible teaches that 'God is love'. In English 'love' is a supermarket word. One can love anything from a spouse or child to an ice cream or a movie. Thankfully the ancient Greeks were more precise. They had separate words for sexual love, familial love, friendship love and so on. In the original Greek New Testament there is a separate, special word for Christian love. It is *agape*. *Agape* is the kind of love that Jesus Christ revealed, especially by his suffering on the cross. *Agape* is the heart of the Christian moral life, summed up in Jesus Christ's two great *agape* commandments. He said:

> *Love the Lord your God with all your heart, with all your soul, with all your mind, and with all your strength. Love your neighbour as you love yourself. There is no other commandment more important than these two* (Mark 12:30-31).

But what is *agape*? In a beautiful hymn of praise St Paul defined it like this:

> *Love is patient; love is kind and envies no one. Love is never boastful, nor conceited, nor rude; never selfish, not quick to take offence. Love keeps no score of wrongs; does not gloat over other men's sins, but delights in the truth. There is nothing love cannot face; there is no limit to its faith, its hope, and its endurance. Love will never come to an end* (1 Corinthians 13:4-8).

Despite the dreamy sentimentality of romantic songs and poems, there is only one real reason why love can never come to an end — because God is love. Which is not to say that love is God. There is something of God in all love. But as every love-smothered child and every love-affair thrill-seeker knows, without *agape* love, love soon turns demonic.

Love is not a word or an idea; love is a power. Christianity says creation itself flowed out of God's love. Christ's mission to rescue our fallen existence came streaming from the love of God. The power of love is not an empty religious cliche. We know it in ordinary everyday life too. And we, who can will love's opposite, know also the power of hate. Psychologists tell us that parent-bashed children are prone to become in turn children-bashing parents.

There is a man who tells this story about the power of accepting love. He was once an alcoholic. Addiction was ruining his career, his marriage and his family. His wife and teenage children nagged him to take control of himself. Eventually they fell to accusation and blame, slowly growing to hate him as the cause of their great unhappiness. He wanted to stop drinking, but he could not. Every failure, every new domestic scene of hate and blame, pushed him deeper into self-hate and more drink. He used verbal aggression and occasional physical violence to hide his inner self-loathing from the family's view. But these tactics only served to increase the circle of hate. The family was Baptist and the pastor frequently visited their home. But not once did the pastor advise, chide or blame the man for his alcoholism. He simply offered friendship and casual conversation. One day the man went to see the pastor privately at his home. For the first time he broke down and confessed his self-hate and his longing to be free from drink. He says the pastor's loving acceptance was the power which began to strengthen a will now totally free from the chains of alcoholic addiction. He has no reproaches to make against his family. He says they were caught in his own circle of self-destruction.

The inner mystic presence of the Holy Spirit tells us we are fully accepted by God. The pastor's acceptance of the alcoholic gave him enough positive self-image to begin to break the spiral of self-hate. With God's acceptance, we can accept our self in spite of sins, sins and guilt. And like the human love which is its pale reflection, God's love creates the return of love. As St John says, 'We love God because he first loved us'. God's love frees us to love other human beings too, because in one important sense we do not need them anymore.

Jesus Christ's second *agape* command said, 'Love your neighbour as you love yourself'. Sometimes this is interpreted to mean, 'Love your neighbour and hate yourself'. But Jesus did not say this. People who hate themselves, and to some degree all of us do, cannot truly love others. Until we let God's free-forgiving love destroy our guilt, we cannot love our own inner self. And as long as we cannot love our self, we will project a need 'love' on to other people. Need-love and Christian love are opposites.

Need-love often comes from self-hate. It can take the form of power or weakness. In the form of power, need-love seeks to boost the ego by crushing others. Usually it will disguise its need to be needed by appearing aloof and strong. It wants to be admired and will often seem superhuman in its efforts to attain praise. Its tools are humiliation, back-stabbing, controlled gossip, status rituals, verbal assassination and, in the extreme, violence.

As weakness, need-love seeks to boost the hated

self by clammy, cloying, fawning attachment to another. The other is believed worthy and great, whether in fact he or she actually is so. It is not at all uncommon for a weak need-love self to attach its self to a powerful need-love self. Many marriages and political relationships are like this. The tools of weak need-love are 'yes' words, pity-seeking tears, hurt anger, in-group gossip, flattery, snobbery and, in the extreme, suicidal threats. God's love lets us rejoice in what we are and in what others are too. Need-love seeks to find in others what can only be found in God.

No Christian will ever attain perfect *agape* love for God or others in this life. Forgiven, we yet remain sinners. But the perfect circle of love is the destination of the moral journey the Holy Spirit leads us on. I once heard someone describe this journey as a mountain climb. Despite many falls and backward slides down steep slopes, he said, the passing years should bring us nearer the peak. But this is a dangerous picture. People on moral mountains look down on those below. Jesus reserved his sharpest criticism for the religious sin of self-righteous pride.

There is a parable which tells what progress on the Christian moral journey is really like:

> *Once there was a priest with a large public hospital in his parish. Each morning he visited the sick, but they found no comfort from his words. His bedside prayers were cold and mechanical. This priest had always been a healthy man and, except for a childhood tonsillectomy, had never once been ill in*

> *hospital himself. One day the priest was awakened early by excruciating pains in his stomach. He had never imagined such hurt and fear before. The next day his doctor removed three large gall stones. But soon the priest was well again and he resumed his morning round of hospital visits. Patients said they had never met such a kind, gentle priest. He prays, they said, like a saint.*

By casting light upon the murkier depths of the self, the Holy Spirit shows how much we have been forgiven. He shows the thin membrane of social conformity which has kept the adulterer, murderer and thief just below outward projection for most of us. There is no moral mountain here. Instead there is sympathetic vision. Seeing the depths of our own evil, we become gentler with others, even with those who have pierced the membrane and scandalized the self-righteous. We see there are only two kinds of human beings: sinners who have accepted God's loving forgiveness and sinners who have not. The former have nothing to boast about except the love of God. Jesus revealed the secret of Christian moral growth when he spoke about the prostitute convert who washed his feet with her tears and wiped them in thankfulness with her hair. Of this woman Jesus said:

> *I tell you, her great love proves that her many sins have been forgiven; where little has been forgiven, little love is shown* (Luke 7:47).

Christianity and sexual repression

One could easily be excused for thinking Christian morality consisted of little else than sexual morality.

Christians never seem to stop harping about sex. There are good and bad reasons for this. We will look at the bad first.

God took human flesh in the person of Jesus Christ. Thus we might expect Christianity to be a religion which hallowed flesh. Yet much Christianity seems to do the opposite, treating God and flesh as implacable enemies. Why? In part this sad mistake derives from a simple misunderstanding of language, corrected in only the most recent biblical translations.

In St Paul's New Testament letters, flesh and spirit are constantly opposed as opposites. He says Christians must reject the flesh and follow the spirit. Hence critics of Christian sexual morality have tagged Paul with such labels as 'repressed', 'passionless' and 'anti-sex'. Yet here is Paul's list of the kind of behaviour which will ensue from the flesh rather than the spirit:

> *Now the works of the flesh* [Greek sarx] *are immorality, impurity, indecency, idolatry and sorcery, quarrels, a contentious temper, envy, fits of rage, selfish ambitions, dissensions, party intrigues and jealousy, drinking bouts, orgies* (Galatians 5:20-21).

No one could deny this list contains items of sexual immorality, e.g. indecency and orgies. But equally no one could deny that this list of the sins of the flesh mainly consists of mind and non-sexual sins of relationships, e.g. sorcery (seances), rage, temper, selfish ambition etc. Plainly St Paul does not use 'flesh' to mean physical flesh as we do today. Modern translations render Paul's Greek word *sarx* as 'human nature' instead of flesh. St Paul is not thinking of a split within human beings — a kind of lower self (flesh) and a kind of higher self (spirit). But sadly several centuries of mistranslation has caused Christians to take him this way. The split St Paul is thinking of is between us and God. To follow the Spirit means to follow the Holy Spirit. To follow the flesh (*sarx*) means to follow the God-rebellious human will. The latter results in all the sins of evil human nature, both sexual and non-sexual.

The other main source of anti-sex ideas in Christianity is not derived from Christ or the Bible, but from the Greek cultural context of early Christian theology. The Greeks, including Plato, tended to split the self between a higher and lower nature. They viewed matter as base or evil. As early Christian theologians looked around for ideas to explain and interpret their faith, it was natural they should turn to the sophisticated Greek philosophers. Unfortunately they imbibed several quite un-Christian ideas, rejection of the life of human flesh being one of them. This led at least one influential theologian of the early church to castrate himself in order to resist temptation. It also led to the exaltation of virginity as a higher spiritual state than marriage. It is true that Jesus and Paul thought marriage would sometimes interfere with a special Christian vocation, but the reasons were the practical ones of the absence of family responsibilities and ties, not a higher spirituality. Throughout its pages, the Bible hallows the goodness of matter and marriage.

Sex as a substitute for God

But we must turn to the good reasons why Christians talk a lot about sex. First is the danger of allowing sexual, ecstatic mysticism to replace spiritual, ecstatic mysticism. It is no accident that modern Western pre-occupation with sex comes at a time when Christianity is in decline. If we were made to find the completion of our being in a personal relationship with God, then those who reject God will search around for something to take God's place. Sex — with its ecstatic, orgasmic, infinitizing feelings and a long and ancient history of idolatrous connections — is a likely contender.

Not that there is anything the matter with orgasm. Passionate Christians will praise God for orgasm as much as for sunsets or misty mountain mornings. But they will not confuse the red-heat passion of sexual desire (*eros*) with the white-heat passion of spiritual desire (*agape*). They will agree with the biblical writer who said, 'There is a time to embrace and a time to refrain from embracing'.

The time to refrain from embracing is the time when sexual desire begins to supplant spiritual desire. Life is not sex; the orgasmic infinitizing is a spurious infinite, as momentary and finite as the blood through which it courses. True infinity was nailed to the cross to suffer, die and rise again. Suffering and death are obscenities to sexual mystics. Being the ultimate impotence, death is unspeakable. As Carl Jung saw, if we are to be finally healed we must pass from the meaning of the phallic symbol to the meaning of the cross symbol.

Christians are for sex, but they do not mistake sex for God.

The second good reason why Christianity talks a lot about sex is because it believes sex was given to intensify, not lessen, the value of persons. In the Genesis story Adam ('human') is divided into male and female because of the loneliness of the single self. This is the theological source of the Christian view that companionship is the prime reason for marriage.

We saw earlier that in this biblical story the term for sexual-love is 'to know', a personal relationship. Today in Western countries perhaps the most common term is 'to screw', a mechanical relationship. Alone among earth's creatures God made human bodies into transcendent persons. And alone among the bodily creatures God made human genitals for making love face-to-face. Sexual love with its physical coupling and orgasmic ecstasy was made to seal personal knowing. When we 'screw' someone we do not know; sexual love has turned intimate personal knowing into the charade of thing-to-thing.

Christianity says sexual love is for marriage and marriage is a commitment until death. We can fall out of romantic love just as we fell into it in the first place. Christian marriage is based upon *agape* love, not romantic love. After marriage, different life-experiences may cause a husband and wife to grow differently and apart. In advanced industrial societies, with their rapid social changes and rigid sex stereotyping, this is not a vague possibility but almost a certainty.

Some people advocate that every time we change, we should seek a partner attuned to our new 'wave length'. They call it *serial marriage*. But serial marriage is a prescription for the loneliness marriage was given to avoid. Serial marriage is an attempt to find happiness by stepping around suffering. If Christianity is true, the way to any kind of resurrection — including the resurrection of marital happiness — is through, not around suffering. Serial marriage invites us to walk through life totally alone, with a series of broken relationships trailing tragically behind us.

Going through suffering is not the same as wallowing in it or stoically putting up with it. Going through suffering means husband and wife talking together, praying together and adjusting their life patterns so they can start growing together again. *Agape* love will always be dying on a cross, but it will always rise again too.

But this picture is the ideal. Many will get close to it and many will fail miserably. Somehow when they come to the subject of sex or marriage, Christians seem to forget that this is a fallen, twisted, fractured world. This is not meant to say Christians should relinquish their ideal. Rather it is meant to say that Christians should be more consistent in their compassion and forgiveness.

In reality there will be people who cannot raise their dead marriages: people who succumb to adultery's temptation, who grow up homosexual, who long but fail to find a suitable marriage partner. Christians have accepted the principle that in war it may be necessary to kill another person as the lesser of two evils. In this life, *agape* is seldom faced with a clear choice between black and white. It usually has to choose between two shades of grey. All grey is grey, but some grey is nearer to white than black. In sex and marriage, it is high time Christians let *agape* subtly discern between the different shades. Jesus said to the Jews that 'the sabbath was made for man and not man for the sabbath'. Would he say 'marriage was made for man and not man for marriage'? This is a question at least worth pondering.

The third good reason why Christians talk so much about sex is children. No other creature comes into the world so helpless and dependent as a human baby. Failure to nurture our own children is failure to take responsibility for our own freely chosen sexual activity. No one could seriously deny that the greatest gift parents can give a child is a happy marriage. *Agape* love never allows a child to shoulder up the broken arch of an unhappy marriage relationship. Nothing is farther from *agape* love than one parent colluding with a child against another parent. And nothing will twist a child-person more than turning him or her into a surrogate husband or a surrogate wife.

I am not talking about physical incest, though that relatively rare phenomenon is included too. I am talking about psychic incest, where the parent forces the child to give up his/her childhood to become an adult partner. Persons are made in and through their families. Christianity says the family is the basic unit of human society — an obvious truism. But when family life begins to fail, it is a sure sign that the society has lost its religious bearings and is heading towards ruin.

It's easy to cry 'hypocrisy'

One of the most common objections to Christianity has nothing whatever to do with the truth of its theological reality map. The objection is moral — the failure of Christians to live up to their professed ideals. It is no use Christians trying to hedge around this criticism. They must admit as fact that many atheists, humanists and secularists come closer to Christ's ideals than they do. And it is no answer to insist that the essence of Christianity is God's free-forgiving love. Although this is quite true, others will see it as an excuse for moral laxity. People will always judge Christianity by the lives of Christians they know. Christ himself expected and welcomed this test. 'By their fruits you shall know them', he said. But before we condemn Christianity for the paucity of its moral crop, we need to examine the kind of comparisons people make.

At law, humane societies try to take account of a crime's mitigating circumstances. Hence a man who kills someone for a fee will receive a stiffer penalty than a wife who stabs her husband with the kitchen knife in the middle of a violent domestic argument. Even though each act produces the same result, the law distinguishes between degrees of moral responsibility. It recognizes that moral behaviour does not take place in a vacuum.

Moral comparisons which exclude circumstances will accord praise and blame to life situations totally beyond an individual's control. It is unlikely that a girl from a rich family will ever steal a loaf of bread, but a girl from an extremely poor family may steal many loaves. To what degree is one more moral than the other?

Or take two men both of equally genial temper. One has always enjoyed perfect health and the other has crippling arthritis. Do we not suspect that the arthritic has conquered more temptations of bitterness and irritability than the other?

How do we compare the urbane, generous atheist doctor who grew up in a loving, middle-class family circle, with the laconic, shy, somewhat selfish Christian clerk who was the only son of a deserted, alcoholic mother?

The only valid moral comparisons are *self*-comparisons. The atheist doctor may not have risen one moral degree above what circumstances made him. The Christian clerk may have risen one hundred degrees above his circumstances, yet still be far below the doctor in a moral vacuum comparison. Jesus recognized this distinction when he said, 'Everyone to whom much is given, of him will much be required'.

The right question to ask is: Does Christianity make any *difference* to a person's moral behaviour? Would the doctor be a better man if he became a Christian? Is the clerk a better man because he has become a Christian? These are much harder questions to answer than the questions posed by the glib 'moral vacuum' method. But they are the only valid questions. In each case Christianity claims the answer is 'Yes, Christianity *does* make a difference'. Morally speaking, Christianity stands or falls on the truth of this claim.

22

Utopia: Yes, but not yet

CHRISTIAN SOCIAL MORALITY

Karl Marx was quite right to think utopian society would be stateless. In a society where every person loved their neighbours as they loved themselves, there would be no need for the state. But Marx was quite wrong to think human beings could ever achieve utopia here in earth.

Christianity views the state as a necessary evil. Both words are carefully chosen: the state is necessary and evil. It is necessary because human beings are sinful — they do not love their neighbours as they love themselves. Without the fear of state imposed penalties, they will drive through red traffic lights, sell contaminated foods, lie, cheat, steal and murder. If society is not to tear itself apart through selfish, aggressive individualism, its members must be made to act as if they really do love each other.

The state is evil because it is not founded upon love, but coercion and power. Law, not love, is the state's charter. The ultimate power of the state is force: fines, banishment, imprisonment and, in some cases, the death penalty. (Most Christians would resist the idea that the state should have power to impose the death penalty.) But the state's evil is necessary — necessary because the alternative is a greater evil. In a community of sinners, the alternative to the rule of law is anarchy.

This is not to say that all the evils of the state are necessary. The powers of the state are wielded by a group of sinful human beings too. Hence they are very likely to succumb to the temptation to use the powers of the state to serve themselves and their own vested interest groups. No one has exposed the seductive wiles of this temptation more clearly than Karl Marx. But Christianity cannot accept Marx's idealistic social behaviourism which explains the abuse of power as due solely to social structures. Christianity says the problem resides in human sinfulness. Changing the social structures only replaces one sinful group at the top with another sinful group. Marx thought the top itself could be abolished by a new structure. Christians will respond that Marx has mistaken earth for heaven, but more about this in a moment.

It is often said that the Christian community (the Church) should stick to religion and keep out of politics and economics. But that is a nonsense view based on a very narrow-minded idea of religion — let alone of politics and economics. In the last chapter we looked at face-to-face personal relationships in the light of Christian morality. Politics and economics are about personal relationships too — not face-to-face, but social structural relationships.

The great bulk of political and economic decision-making is moral decision-making. We have seen that meaning and ethics are the two great strands of all religion. No Christian can be true to Christianity and remain silent about ethical matters.

Christian social morality will usually be more concerned about ends than means. *Ends* concern social goals — goals such as whether taxes should be levied more heavily upon the rich than the poor; whether going to war against another society is a retaliation against evil aggression or a selfish act of economic imperialism; whether and what amount of social security benefits should be paid to the aged and the sick. Goals always involve love and neighbours; they are always ethical. *Means* can be ethical or just technical. Having decided it is the lesser of two evils to drop bombs on a neighbour, one still has to decide the comparative ethics of TNT, napalm or atomic bombs. But whether X computer will process social security cheques more efficiently than Y computer is a technical question Christians will happily leave to the experts.

Tomorrow affects today

Strange as it may seem, heaven is the most practical idea Christianity can contribute to social morality. Christians see themselves living in the interregnum between God's *yes* and God's *not yet*. God's 'yes' is Christ. What he is and what he did affirms that the ultimate power at the source of all reality is personal and is love. God's 'yes' affirms the coming kingdom of love, when heaven will completely reverse earth's evil. But it will be God's doing, not ours as the Marxists say. And it will happen at the end of human history, not in human history. God's 'not yet' is the continued existence of this present evil world.

We do not know why or how long God's 'not yet' will last. Perhaps the secret is that God will wait to restore all things until human beings have destroyed all things? But how are such ideas practical?

First, because they are the perfect balance between idealism and practical compromise. In our 'not yet' world, there will never be a utopian society, but some societies will be better than others. Christianity has no blueprint for a Christian society such as many Marxists have for a Marxist society. Whatever forms of society help neighbours love each other most (or act as if they do) will gain the support of Christians. In some historical circumstances this might be democracy and market capitalism; in others it might be enlightened monarchy, democracy or socialism. Ideally Christians might favour a combination of democracy and socialism as most likely to produce equal love among neighbours.

But as Christianity knows, ideals seldom work in sinful societies. The moral ideals of democratic socialism often seem to lead to equality in poverty, whereas democratic capitalism, which seems to find its motivations in individual greed, appears to produce more goods for both rich and poor. Of course these comments are very superficial. The main point is that Christians will not cut throats or throw bombs in any vain effort to produce utopia. They will seek compromises that come nearest to the ideal of neighbourly love, never expecting anything more.

Youthful dreams of heaven on earth soon turn into apathetic cynicism in later life. But Christians never become apathetic or cynical about social reform. God's 'yes' is a charter for idealism. Every day Christians pray, 'Thy will be done on earth as it is in heaven'. Believing they can never fully achieve what they pray for, Christians will nevertheless act as if they can, because they believe God ultimately will. This is the balance which avoids unrealistic idealism (with its petrol bombs and cut throats) and an apathetic cynicism (which retires to write satire or watch football).

The second reason why heaven is such a practical concept for social morality is because it provides a fearless vantage point for judging the actions of earthly rulers. Of course the ideal would be that all earthly rulers themselves act with a consciousness of heaven's judgment. But even more than the rest of us, political rulers want others to think that their ideas and actions reflect some inalterable condition of reality itself and are therefore beyond question or criticism.

A parent who says to a child, 'You must not pick your nose in public' will carry much less weight than a parent who says, 'One does not pick one's nose in public'. The first parent speaks only with personal authority; the second seems to have the whole human race, even the cosmos itself, supporting the ban on public nose-picking.

Political rulers like to give the impression their rules are cosmological too. In the past they made claims to divinity or divine right; nowadays they are more likely to claim that they represent racial superiority, historic destiny or the true spirit of the age. Apart from a few unhappy exceptions — hang-overs from the past — Christianity is no longer used to give cosmological legitimation to the state. Christians will respect the state, but they will not confuse earthly rulers with the heavenly ruler. In secular and Marxist societies, the Christian community is fast becoming one of the few vantage points from which people can stand back and evaluate the state by external standards.

Social structures can kill

Face-to-face evil is usually willed and unavoidably self-conscious. It is hard to avoid a sense of guilt when we lie to friends, steal from an employer or bash our children in anger. But one of the subtleties of social or structural evil is the possibility of participating in it without being conscious of committing sin at all.

For example, how many North Americans are conscious that they use more fertilizer on their lawns, gardens and golf courses each year than starving India uses for food production? Or how many white Australians realize their long history of racism has pushed the one-percent black minority into urban and rural slums where Aboriginal infant mortality is up to 600% higher than for whites? Individual Americans or Australians do not murder Indians or Aborigines, but they participate in *structural* relationships which are as deadly as poison or guns. Christian morality is always personal, whether the relationships are face-to-face or social-structural. Christianity cannot accept the view that young radicals are morally upright so long as they oppose racism or environmental pollution, but neglect their parents or sleep around indiscriminately. Nor can it accept the morality of their conservative elders who assume they are morally upright so long as they avoid lies, adultery and alcoholism, but are blind to reaping profits from companies that pollute the atmosphere or exploit the poor.

Social structures are human projections — we create them communally. Unlike the material universe, they have no existence apart from us. If every human being on earth died, there would be no children's birthday parties, no economic system, no governments, no schools and no banks. But if every human being on earth dies, we can imagine that gravity, Mars and Mt Everest would still be here, although no human beings would be here to observe them.

It follows that social structures are only evil because of the evil of their human creators. Perfect human beings would project perfect social structures. Marxists are wrong to think that social evils will ever be eliminated simply by creating new structures. Unless we can eliminate the evil in the human will, new structures will only reflect the evil of their creators. That is why Christianity places so much emphasis on the need for individual, spiritual rebirth. But there is a partial truth in what Marxists have to say about social structures.

It is true that social structures do tend to take on an evil of their own. A superficial, but frightening example is the mob riot. Perfectly ordinary people get caught up in a mob situation, say a riot at a political rally or a football match, where they do things that afterwards they can hardly believe. The chaos of war or the mob hysteria whipped up by movements like Nazism have even more frightening effects. But Christianity does not blame the structures. What happens in these cases is that the depth of evil in each ordinary human heart is suddenly released from the social conventions that usually keep it just below the surface. This is why, when evil social structures need change, Christianity generally favours reform, not revolution. By shattering the delicate fibres of normal social conventions, revolution takes the lid off the demonic depths within human beings. To get that lid back on usually requires a rule of force as bad or worse than the evils the revolution was supposed to solve.

A more profound example of social structures taking on an evil life of their own is their historical tendency to institutionalize evil. Each of us is born into a world which already has massive social structures — the projections of our forbears. These structures, forming subtle weaves of family, wealth, social class and national identity, largely make us what we become. We make history, but we are mostly made by it. Thus our forbears' evil has an enormously strong tendency to preserve itself from generation to generation. Social background can become one of the greatest obstacles to letting God form a Christian conscience in us.

I once knew a devout Christian medical doctor who was as intelligent as anyone I have ever met. He came from a wealthy, upper-class English family which regarded all non-Europeans as distinctly inferior. On one occasion he tried to persuade me that the biblical creation stories explained the origin of the European race and evolution explained the origin of all the others. Europeans, he said, were created by God after his own image and likeness. Non-Europeans descended from apes and were not spiritual beings or really human at all.

This example is extreme, but not exceptional. It shows how evil social structures can so mould a child that even intelligence and adult conversion to Christianity can fail to eliminate sinful prejudice.

It is nonsense to claim that all men are born equal. It would be truer to say that all human beings die equally. But silver-decorated coffins and elaborate mausoleums give a certain lie even to that claim. Apart from the inequalities of genetically inherited intelligence or physical strength, evil social structures ensure that human beings are born anything but equal. Some are born into grinding poverty and some are born into wealth and luxury. There is only one true sense in which human beings are equal: they are equal in the sight of God — equal before his love and therefore equal before his judgment too.

In God's eyes, probably the greatest moral scandal of the modern era is the structural relationship which allows one-third of the world's population to live like kings while the other two-thirds barely live at all. Christians must see that bread for themselves is a material and physical question, but bread for their starving neighbours is a moral and spiritual question.

* * *

This is the end of a book about a journey home. The way is both mystical and moral — in that order. The mystical way guides thought and feeling; the moral way guides action and doing. In every thought, reverie, ecstasy and dream, in every spoken word and action, we are either coming closer to home or drifting further away. What we are is what we do, and what we do becomes what we are.

Old age is a test. What shall we be then? Will each new day be savoured for its own delicacy and each person treated with growing gentleness? Or will the self be ashen and bitter, filled with selfish concern about fading health and powers? Either we allow our being to incorporate itself into God or let the passing years slowly render our lives ever more ragged and inconsequential. Either this present passage of temporal fact becomes fused into God, or it drifts inexorably into its own private nightmare.

We live in an era of outward journeying which has achieved unprecedented material power. But material power has not diminished the fundamental finitude, mystery and guilt of being human. Every family doctor, parish priest or taxi-driver knows this far better than most of our scientists, theologians and philosophers.